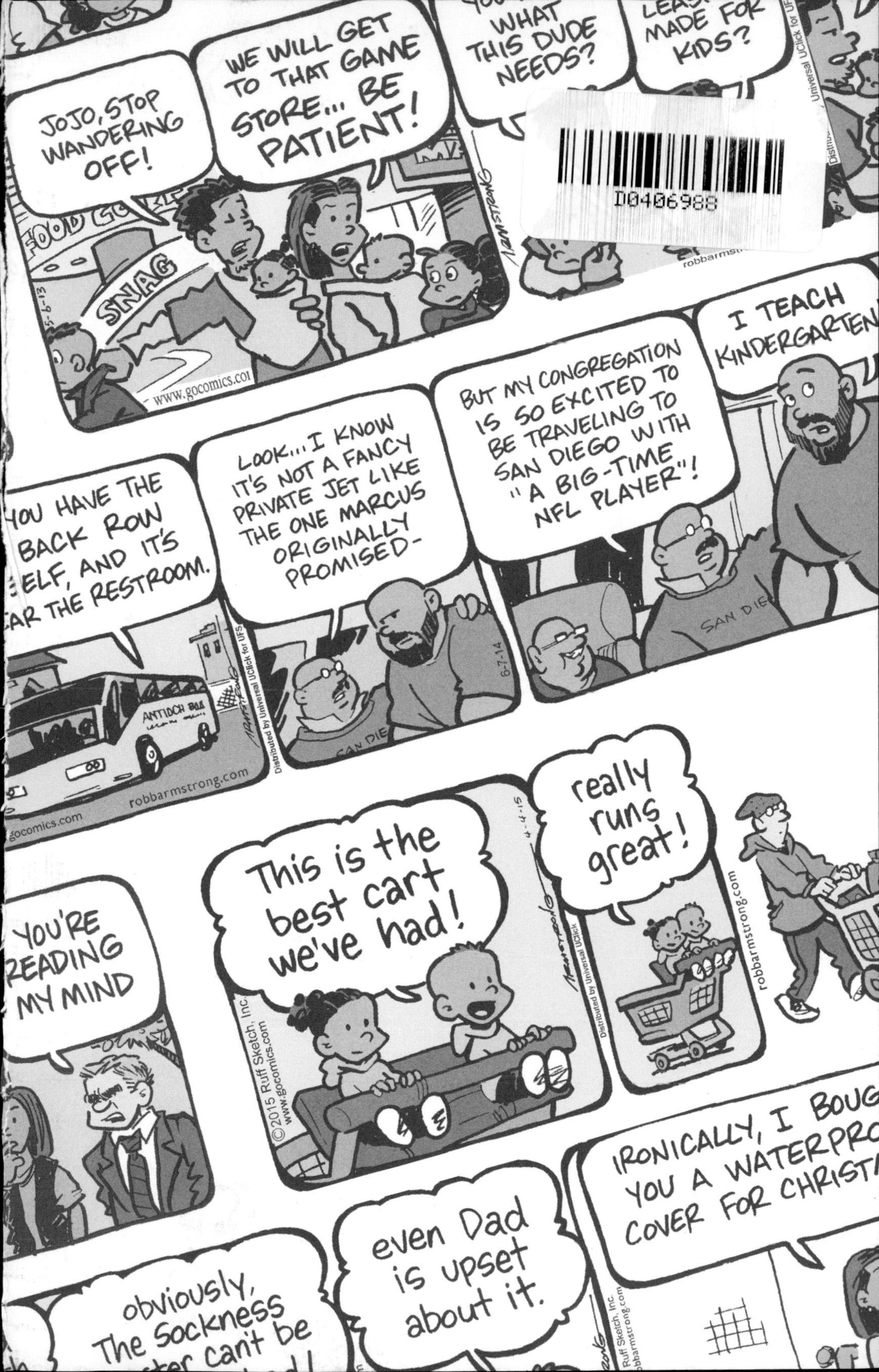
JOJO, STOP WANDERING OFF!
WE WILL GET TO THAT GAME STORE... BE PATIENT!
WHAT THIS DUDE NEEDS?
MADE FOR KIDS?
FOOD
SNAG
5-6-13
www.gocomics.com
robbarmstrong.com
I TEACH KINDERGARTEN
BUT MY CONGREGATION IS SO EXCITED TO BE TRAVELING TO SAN DIEGO WITH "A BIG-TIME NFL PLAYER"!
LOOK... I KNOW IT'S NOT A FANCY PRIVATE JET LIKE THE ONE MARCUS ORIGINALLY PROMISED-
YOU HAVE THE BACK ROW
ELF, AND IT'S
AR THE RESTROOM.
ANTIOCH BIA
6-7-14
SAN DIE
Distributed by Universal UClick for UFS
robbarmstrong.com
gocomics.com
really runs great!
This is the best cart we've had!
4-4-15
YOU'RE READING MY MIND
©2015 Ruff Sketch, Inc.
www.gocomics.com
Distributed by Universal UClick
robbarmstrong.com
IRONICALLY, I BOUG
YOU A WATERPRO
COVER FOR CHRIST
even Dad is upset about it.
obviously, The Sockness
can't be
Ruff Sketch, Inc.
robbarmstrong.com

A Cartoonist's Guide to Life

ROBB ARMSTRONG

Reader's
digest

New York / Montreal

A READER'S DIGEST BOOK

Copyright © 2016 by Ruff Sketch, Inc.

JumpStart comic strips reprinted in this book are copyright of Ruff Sketch, Inc., distributed by Universal Uclick. All other images in this book are reprinted courtesy of Robb Armstrong, with the exception of the images on the following pages: 11 Shutterstock; 81, 84, and 86 (left) Barbara Clothier; 86 (right) Howard Hurtig; 106 King Features; 110 Victor della Barbara; 119 Jean Schulz; 120 Sarah Ashman Gillespie; 141 Khalil Postell; 161 John Trombetta; 196 Bridget McMeel; 198 Wendi Niad; 199 Nikita Adams; 208 Scott Allen/PR Photos.

ISBN 978-1-62145-287-4/Epub ISBN 978-1-62145-288-1

Library of Congress Cataloging-in-Publication Data
Names: Armstrong, Robb, author.
Title: Fearless : a cartoonist's guide to life / Robb Armstrong.
Description: New York : Reader's Digest, 2016.
Identifiers: LCCN 2015042669 | ISBN 9781621452874 (hardback)
Subjects: LCSH: Armstrong, Robb. | Cartoonists–United States–Biography. | African American cartoonists–Biography. | BISAC: BIOGRAPHY & AUTOBIOGRAPHY / Personal Memoirs. | HUMOR / Form / Comic Strips & Cartoons. | BIOGRAPHY & AUTOBIOGRAPHY / Artists, Architects, Photographers.
Classification: LCC PN6727.A6857 Z46 2016 | DDC 741.5/973–dc23
LC record available at http://lccn.loc.gov/2015042669

We are committed to both the quality of our products and the service we provide to our customers. We value your comments, so please feel free to contact us.

Reader's Digest Trade Publishing
44 South Broadway
White Plains, NY 10601

For more Reader's Digest products and information, visit our website:
www.rd.com (in the United States)
www.readersdigest.ca (in Canada)

Printed in China

10 9 8 7 6 5 4 3 2 1

Crystal, Rex, Tess

My life. My purpose.

CONTENTS

ACKNOWLEDGMENTS

Many people made sacrifices to get me where I am today—people I know, and people I've never met. Some are Black, some white. Even God in heaven sacrificed for me. It isn't enough to say, "Thanks, I'm grateful." I have to be willing to sacrifice for others if I'm grateful. And I have to do it seeking nothing in return.

If you're going through hell, keep going.
—Winston Churchill

INTRODUCTION:
I DRAW THE FUNNIES

I'm a cartoonist. I fell in love with drawing when I was three, and I've been penning *JumpStart*, an award-winning comic strip about everyday family life, for more than two decades. My life has been a long journey, full of exhilarating moments and depressing events. Sometimes I feel that I have succeeded despite myself, despite my fears of the many, many unknowns I have faced.

I've been called lucky, but I do not subscribe to notions of luck. Life can be terrifying. Uncertainty can freeze you in your tracks like a deer in headlights. You must rely on more than luck. You must become fearless. I hope the life lessons and art lessons in this book will help reveal the fearlessness inside you.

I owe a debt of gratitude to my mother, my siblings, my friends, my teachers, and my wife, Crystal. But I would also credit several personal, internal constants in my life. I have a passion, and I never wavered in pursuing it, even when sidetracked by school, jobs, or life's daily distractions. And I had God sitting on my shoulder, helping me through some terrible events that could have easily derailed me.

You have your own path to pursue, your own dream, and your own set of obstacles in your way. I hope, in this book and with my example, to give you some added fortitude, some comfort in your bad times, some sense that, if I could succeed, you can, too.

And perhaps we can have some fun along the way. My comic strip, *JumpStart*, revolves around ordinary people facing life's daily challenges with a good dose of humor.

My strip is nationally syndicated in the *Philadelphia Inquirer*, the *New York Daily News*, the *Boston Globe*, the *Los Angeles Times*, and more than four hundred

With Judi, my mom, and Snoopy in 1969.

other publications reaching upward of eighty million readers across the globe daily, including Sundays. I also do individual cartoons for the likes of the *New Yorker* magazine and others—extremely difficult markets to break into.

I'm one of a handful of African-American comic-strip artists to reach an audience of this size. I make people laugh. I point out hilarious truisms. As far as I'm concerned, I've got the best job in the world.

Which means my life is pretty good, too. While I have daily deadlines, I get to work flexible hours, allowing me to spend time with my wife and my two children. I travel around the country, speaking to young people in high schools and colleges, teaching drawing and art, and sharing stories about my life and my journey. I've even met my share of famous people, including my idol, Charles Schulz, whose *Peanuts* comic strip so inspired me as a kid, and who became a good friend in his final years. And I've enjoyed the financial and professional accolades that come with success.

There are many people who may be on their way toward success but will never achieve it. I don't know them by name, and neither do you. They might have made it if they hadn't let fear get in their way.

West Philadelphia, where I was born and raised, was rugged, and my mother raised five children on her own. My father abandoned all of us when I was born. We lived in a cramped apartment where the electric bill didn't always get paid.

It almost sounds like a cliché, and it would be only a cliché if nothing had been learned from it—if my hardships had turned me into a statistic. But that is not what happened. What happened was miraculous!

With the support of some wonderful people, a lot of hard work and courage, and even more mistakes and laughter, I fought through the hard times and made quite a happy life for myself. But there is more to life than personal happiness. As it turns out, my story has a greater theme. It can be repurposed to help anyone who has the courage to apply some lessons to their own life's journey. (Which reminds me of an old saying: If all else fails, you can always serve as a horrible example. It's true, in my case. I haven't always been the example to follow. But if you're going through fire, follow someone who knows how to get to the other

Here I am (on the far right), twenty-two years later, sitting next to my idol, *Peanuts* creator Charles Schulz. Also having dinner with us are the late Mark Cohen, a well-known comic-strip collector (far left), and *Dilbert* creator Scott Adams (middle left).

side.) Yes, you can succeed—no matter what is happening in your life right now, no matter how afraid you may be of the unknown—if you accept help from those around you and celestial help from above, and you have the grit to see the sunrise at the end of the darkness.

I certainly did.

And I did it by drawing funnies.

Life is not so different from the comics, you know: the challenges, tragedies, and triumphs. Comics poke fun at our everyday routines and our universal motivations. They show us a lot about ourselves and offer little windows into the people and lessons we don't yet understand.

In my own comic strips, I show the joys of falling in love and the no-holds-barred battles of the heart. I capture loss and memories. I draw the thrill of becoming a parent and the pain of failing my kids. Drawing affects me, and my life experiences affect the drawings. Drawing helps me to see things differently. It gives me a deeper perspective on life. The artist is not a person who draws; the

artist is a person who sees what other humans cannot. So, as a cartoonist, I have drawn a few lessons from life to share with you.

Because my strip is published every day without repeats, the hardest part about my job is meeting relentless deadlines. In 2015, I took a week off to celebrate my birthday with my wife and some friends in Las Vegas. It was the first time *JumpSstart* ran repeats in twenty-six years! I've since learned to relax a bit more with vacations and long weekends. But a career this long is in no small part due to my secret weapon:

Problems!

Trouble, complication, tragedy, adversity—call it whatever you want. In my case, mo' problems means mo' inspiration, mo' drawing, and mo' money.

Everyone has problems, and every good cartoon starts with a problem. First, I come up with an issue—layoffs, family squabbles, relationship conflicts—and then I make fun of the characters going through the problem, or of the problem itself. I do not need to resolve the conflict. I just need to expose the irony of it.

The formula works like a charm—in art and in life.

Drawing can help you overcome your problems, too. (No, you don't need to have any artistic skills. I promise.)

Marcy's Working Late (acrylic on wood, 2007).

One thing I've learned: art, love, and wisdom are worth nothing unless you give them away. Never hold back your best stuff for later. You might not have a later. Give it all away—every bit of it—to your readers, your audience, your partner, and your kids. Give the world your all, and the world will reward you, often in the most unexpected ways.

Fearless is based upon my journey as an artist, father, husband, son, and friend. It is not a book about conquering phobias; it's about achieving your life's purpose despite scary circumstances and formidable opposition.

Each chapter begins with a simple drawing lesson. Artists have a freedom others do not enjoy. Our society shackles people to different things: drugs, jobs they hate, bad relationships, and so on. The drawing lessons in this book offer you a new way of looking at the world and experiencing its beauty and challenges.

Art can be therapeutic and a great alternative to unhealthy obsessions. In a moment of self-doubt or weakness, pick up a pen, a paintbrush, or a glob of clay, and you may discover your own ability to make sense out of confusion and add something beautiful to the world in the process. Art, after all, doesn't die when we die. It lives on and never stops communicating its message to people who gaze upon it, read it, sing it, or dance to it.

The only requirement is that you come with an open mind, an open heart, a desire to learn more about yourself, and a willingness to get more out of life— more inspiration, more satisfaction, more happiness.

After the drawing lesson, I weave in personal experiences and stories, from art, childhood, manhood, and fatherhood.

Last, I add a personal note of inspiration to each chapter.

The book is illustrated with some of my favorite *JumpStart* strips as well as original cartoons created specifically for this book.

Because—hey—I'm a cartoonist. And sometimes a picture is worth a thousand words.

BEFORE YOU START

Some painting supplies aren't cheap. After all, they can be used to create priceless works of art. Art supply stores are big these days, overwhelming, with a large variety for every budget. Ask for assistance, which will cut down the confusion and get you in and out of the store fast. I list the items suggested for each chapter's art lesson. In an appendix there is a full list of art supplies needed. Take that with you when you go shopping.

Chapter 1

IF ROBBIN LIVES, HE WILL BE MENTALLY HANDICAPPED

DRAWING LESSON:
Make a drawing of yourself.

WHAT YOU WILL NEED FOR THIS ART LESSON:

- Pad of tracing paper, 11x14-inch or larger, and larger is better. I use 14x17-inch sheets. Comes in pads or boxes of loose sheets from 50 to 500. One brand comes in a roll like paper towels. Buy a small quantity (50 or so) to start.

- Flair pen (in black). Ball-point pens are no good. Flair is a brush-type that goes on wet and dries almost instantly. As you will see, it's my favorite.

THE LESSON

Self-portraits are hard to do, even for the most accomplished artists. So it probably seems unfair that I've told you to draw yours, and made it the very first drawing lesson. But the point of asking you to draw your face isn't to give you renewed appreciation for Rembrandt, but rather to get you to really look at yourself, and to study your features. When you carefully examine your outer self, you can better understand your inner self.

For example, when I look in the mirror, I see my mouth. I'm all about the mouth—my loud, communicative, laughing mouth. My mouth expresses my mind. It expresses my heart with a kiss. It curses to express anger. Through the mouth, I feed my body.

When you look into the mirror, what do *you* see? Take your time. If you're unsure, this book will help you better understand who you are and what motivates you. I also hope that it will inspire you to be your best possible self, no matter what your circumstances in life.

Look at your face again. Notice that no matter how still you try to hold your features, you can't do it. Beneath the stillness there is always motion. It's likely subtle. Perhaps your lip twitches, your nostrils flare, or your cheeks expand ever so slightly as you inhale. But as long as you are alive, you are always in motion.

I suggest a self-portrait that is expressionless and straight-on. Your drawing will be executed on at least two layers of paper. On the first sheet, you will draw guidelines. Guidelines are rough horizontal and vertical lines—a big plus sign if you will—that help you to place your features on the landscape of your face. On the next sheet, you will use tracing paper to draw a more finished looking piece of artwork.

Begin by figuring out the overall shape of your face. Is it like an oval, a circle, a square, or a triangle? Let's take a look in the mirror:

An oval face is (slightly) wider through the cheekbones, narrowing at hairline and jaw.

A round face is much like the oval but more wide across the cheekbones. Hold your forefingers and thumbs together to make a circle and look through this at your face in the mirror. Does your face touch the circle all the way around?

A square face is much like the round face, but at top and bottom more of the face is touching the circle.

Triangular faces come in two types. The most common is the "jowly" sort, where your cheeks sag a bit so the base of the triangle is at the bottom. But some people start life with a wider forehead and small, narrow chin and are sort of "inverted" triangles.

Now draw your basic geometric shape.

Your face is divided into four quadrants. Draw a vertical line right down through the middle of your head. Then, at the eyeline—right below the eyebrow level—draw a horizontal line.

Next, draw the outline of your hairstyle. This need not be precise. The important thing to note is the distance from your hairline to your eye-

brows. Getting this as accurate as possible is key to creating a good likeness.

Next, draw in your eyebrows right above your horizontal guideline. Pay close attention to the distance between your eyebrows. Take your time with this detail.

To draw your eyes, consider first your eye color. It is not necessary to use colored pencils or pens to draw different-colored eyes. You can use a lighter touch with your black pen to indicate light-colored (blue) eyes, and a heavier touch to indicate dark-colored (brown) eyes. See the example on the next page.

Your personality is evident in your eyes, with your eyelids draping your eyes in a unique way. Even if you don't execute your eyes perfectly, the patience you put into drawing them should result in a self-portrait that looks and feels right.

Your nose has a bridge that starts at your eyebrows and goes from there

almost to your top lip. Your nose is longer and wider than you think. It's somewhat complex, made up of cartilage and soft tissue, and is sometimes an area of the face the owner would like to change. When it comes to drawing self-portraits, this can become a special challenge. If you have always hated your nose or you have scars, I encourage you to be artistically honest. Draw what is there without caricaturing yourself (exaggerating your perceived flaws for the sake of self-mockery).

Simply draw yourself as if you were a model. Try to be as objective as possible.

The tracing paper allows you to make mistakes. Don't throw away failure. Look at it, and learn from it. Use a clean sheet of tracing paper whenever you feel the need to. I love using many layers of tracing paper to slowly arrive at a desired look. But be patient. Art is never a sprint, but a casual stroll while smelling a lot of roses!

If you find that you have multiple versions of your nose, for example, you may find that pausing from this exercise and walking away for a while is helpful. Go run an errand or walk the dog. When you return to your project, it is remarkable how "fresh eyes" bring clarity! Now you may need a fresh layer of paper to get your nose right!

Now draw your chin. Your chin's distance from that bottom lip is key. If you put too much or too little space between your bottom lip and your chin, your final art simply will not look like you.

Examine the geometric shape of your chin. It is its own shape, meaning a person with a triangular head may have an oval chin. Touch it while looking into a mirror. Feel its shape? Add that shape to your drawing. It is one shape. Nobody really has more than one chin. If you have jowls, that was assessed when you decided upon the overall shape of your head.

Now draw your top lip. The right width is key to a good likeness. Your mouth is wide. If you are an adult, unless you have a small mouth, it extends almost across your entire face. Next comes your bottom lip. It has a different shape and attitude than your top lip. Your lips resemble each other but are far from twins. The top lip may be different in color than your bottom lip.

Now add those freckles, laugh lines, and other distinguishing traits.

You are now ready to do your second sheet, this one a tracing over the original rough template. The template started with your guidelines and is now your pattern, much as a seamstress uses a pattern to make a coat. The moment you put that clean sheet on top of this template, you will see what works and what doesn't. If you want to make any fixes on the template page, now is the time!

Trace what works well; ignore what doesn't. Don't get hung up on every strand of hair. Your hairstyle is actually a geometric shape, a polygon that constantly changes. Eyebrows and eyelashes should be executed using short motions to indicate hair and not straight, unbroken lines, or your face will have an unnatural look, like a mannequin.

Do not overwork this self-portrait. You can always draw another one later, if you'd like. Your completed work should be preserved no matter what. It is a reflection of you, created by the person who knows you best!

Now take one more look at your face in the mirror. What do you see? Are you happy with who you are? Who are you, exactly?

MY LIFE: WEST PHILLY

When I was born in 1962, I was diagnosed with encephalitis or "mumps of the brain," a severe form of the common childhood disease. My mother was alarmed and, as it turned out, with good reason. She took me to the doctor, who told her there was nothing that could be done for me.

"He's going to die as a child," the doctor told her. "Even if he lives, he'll be severely retarded." In 1962, even doctors found nothing wrong with using the word retarded.

My mother was not one to accept this prognosis as gospel. She was angered by it and went for a second opinion. (It may sound corny, but always seek a second opinion.) She took me to Philadelphia General Hospital. There, they drained fluid out of my brain and tapped my spine, and the condition went away.

I've enjoyed a healthy life since. Every time I suck in oxygen today, I thank God that my mother was determined enough to welcome me, love me, and care for me. Consider: she already had four kids ranging from four to ten years old by the time I arrived. She was separated from my dad, and life was not easy.

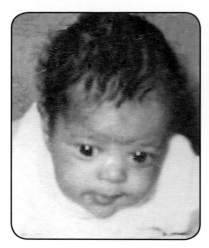

Me as a baby, around two or three
months old.

My mom, Dot, who was pregnant with me at
the time, and siblings in 1961. From left to
right: Cheryle, Billy, Mark, Judi, Mom.

I was born in North Philadelphia, but soon after my birth my family moved to 56th and Walnut in West Philadelphia. My mother, Dorothy "Dot" Armstrong, raised five kids in an apartment in a brick row house over a real estate office. There was no green space. Nothing grew in that neighborhood but the kids. Businesses with apartments over them lined the street, a wall of brick from one intersection to the next, with only the occasional narrow access to tiny backyard areas that had clotheslines, discarded rusting tricycles, dirt, and no grass. Walnut Street was a wide, busy thoroughfare. I was not allowed to go across it without holding someone's hand.

A person would have to walk east, toward Center City, for miles, to see a white man or woman. The nearby "El," or elevated subway train, rumbled in the background, the sound attenuated by distance. The Bond Bakery, which supplied baked goods to area restaurants, was a few blocks north of us, on the corner of 56th and Market, and though this was definitely "the ghetto," it always smelled delicious in my neighborhood.

We were a tight-knit family, and my mother made sure that we stuck together. My father lived somewhere in the Philadelphia area, but I didn't see him. He had abandoned us about the time I was born. It may seem odd that I didn't miss him, but I was so wrapped in love that I didn't even know I was supposed to have a father until somewhat later. I saw fathers in other families, but it took quite some time for it to sink in that the Armstrongs were somehow different. And I can't say that I missed having a father. In fact, sometimes my childhood friends would say they envied me because their fathers beat on them.

Me and my siblings in 1965, when I was three. From left to right: Billy, Judi, me, Mark, Cheryle.

My sister Cheryle was ten years older than I and often looked after me when Mom was not home. Cheryle shouldered much of the burden of raising the family. In the photo above, she is only about fourteen, but looks mature. She sacrificed her high-school fun to make sure we were taken care of.

Billy was seven years older than I, and he was my boyhood hero. He was a "wild child," fearless and adventurous.

Mark was five years older, quiet and introverted. Last, my sister Judi was four years older than I. She was hot-headed and unpredictable, protective of me, her precious baby brother.

While I loved all of my siblings, Billy became my hero early on. It was bath time, and I was around eighteen months old. Judi, age four, was already in the bathtub when my mother told her to move over, that I'd be sharing her bath. It doesn't take great wisdom to know that the last thing a four-year-old girl wants is a toddler in the tub with her, especially when the toddler is still crapping in his diapers! But my mother insisted. She told Judi to keep an eye on me for a moment while she stepped out of the bathroom.

That's when my sister decided to drown me.

Or, if you want to give her the benefit of the doubt, that's when Judi decided it was a fine time to teach me how to swim.

Judi held my head underwater so long that by the time my mom returned to the bathroom, I wasn't breathing and my belly was fully distended and filled with water. When Judi realized this, she let out a yell.

Needless to say, my mother freaked. She pulled me out of the tub. She pushed on my chest, trying to rid me of water and fill me with air. I can only imagine the kind of screaming that took place. It was apparently loud enough that my brother Billy came running into the bathroom. While my mother continued to push on my chest, causing the water to spout from my belly into the air, like a miniature whale, Billy bopped my sister.

Yup. He clocked her good. Now, I'm not advocating fistfights between siblings, or between anyone else for that matter, but if anyone ever deserved a pop upside the head, Judi did then.

I think it's safe to say that Billy became my hero that day.

It's not always easy being the youngest kid, and as the newest and smallest of a six-person family, I had a hard time getting a word in edgewise. That, in turn, made me stutter. When you're told by your (slightly) older siblings to shut up every time you try to join the family conversation, you tend to shut up. My stuttering was certainly an emotional rather than physical problem. Afraid to speak up, I was relieved to turn inward and express myself in artwork instead. Later, once I achieved a measure of success as a middle-school kid at ten or eleven, the stuttering went away. To this day, however, I tend to think about what I'm about to say—but that's not a bad habit anyway.

Mom loved all of us unconditionally. It now seems almost inconceivable to me how a single mother could have given us all that attention and love. Mother, Dot, "Miss Dot" was an incredible person. We were poor and always needed money, and yet Mom would volunteer for things, teaching sewing to the Girl Scouts, and being the neighborhood block captain, for instance. She demon-

Cheryle, Mom, and Judi in 1979.

strated that, no matter how much or how little you have, be generous with it. Bread upon the waters, perhaps; what you give away will come back to enrich you somehow.

I felt honored, even as a kid, to be someone who knew her well. She had legions of friends. I was never able to be quite like her, able to meet a person and immediately cement a lifelong friendship. She was gifted with that ability. People who met her fell in love with her for life.

We never had a car. We didn't need one. People would give us rides. Mom was so confident in this that we would catch public transit to go grocery shopping, and by the time we were done, someone was yelling from a nearby checkout line, "Dot, what's going on?" and then give us a ride home.

When rides with friends were not available, we'd hop back onto the bus with all our stuff. My mom enjoyed the bus and had SEPTA (Southeastern Pennsylvania Transportation Authority) figured out completely. Back then, public transportation could take us anywhere, even on vacation. If SEPTA couldn't do it, Greyhound would. We sometimes went out to New Hope, a small town outside of Philly, on one-day "vacations," or to Smith's Memorial Playground in Fairmount Park just across the Schuylkill River, where they had a giant slide. I loved that place!

I had no idea I was growing up poor. Mom sacrificed for us. She fed us and then went to bed hungry. This turns out to be the recipe for love, period. If you don't self-sacrifice, a relationship is superficial. Kids are smart. They know when a parent sacrifices for them.

Mom's sacrifice came at a price, though. When I was five going on six, she was hospitalized for months with double pneumonia, a dangerous and often-fatal condition where your lungs fill with fluid.

Life Lesson: Don't seek money; seek purpose.

We all have unique strengths and purposes in life. The reason Dot Armstrong garnered so much love and respect is that she was constantly contributing, giving of herself to the community. While other people chased money, she volunteered for things. She gave of herself.

In order to know your strength and purpose, you need to know yourself. Figure out what you were put on Earth to do, *and do that.*

It's not easy. We're often distracted by problems and changes. All of life is in constant motion, and we are, too.

On the upside, since we are constantly moving, that means problems can be temporary, too. Our feelings and our circumstances will always change. It's important that we allow them to flow through us and around us, and deal with pressing issues immediately and fearlessly.

You may be surprised to find that the strong, resilient face in the mirror is yours!

I AM SAVED
BY FRED FLINTSTONE

DRAWING LESSON:
Draw yourself as a cartoon character.

WHAT YOU WILL NEED:

- Photo of yourself; the bigger your face in the photo the better

- Pad of drawing paper suitable for charcoal and pen-and-ink. Comes in pads, often spiral-bound so you keep all your drawings together. I use a 24x36-inch pad, but just get the largest size you can find in the art supply store. Strathmore paper is very good.

- Flair pen

THE LESSON

Look closely at the photo of yourself. Recall the drawing lesson from Chapter 1 and identify the geometric shapes that make up your face. The same shapes make up all of our faces. We are circles, ovals, squares, triangles, and rectangles, and combinations of those. Cartoon character faces, heads, and bodies are created using extreme versions of the shapes.

Is your head more like Charlie Brown or more like SpongeBob Square-Pants? If you think you look like a Minion, then have some fun and draw yourself as one of the Minions! You will definitely have an advantage in this exercise if you've ever been told that you resemble some cartoon character.

When drawing your cartoon self, remember the lessons from drawing your real self. Do not give yourself a round head if the real you has a square head.

If you have far-spaced eyes, draw one eye on a separate sheet of trac-

ing paper. Now overlay the two and move the one eye around until you arrive at a resemblance that is a fun cartoon of you!

Facial hair makes cartoon characters fun and easy. A guy with a big white beard and a portly frame can usually chuckle at his own resemblance to Santa Claus. But make you your own cartoon self, your own doppelgänger.

Amazingly, you will see a unique character emerging right before your eyes. This is the magic of cartooning—and why I love it so! Your creation came from *you*, and not something you've seen on television, or in the funnies. And it was as simple as putting geometric shapes together.

Experiment with expressions on your character's face. Make your character surprised or sad, laughing or angry. It's all in the eyes, which is why cartoon characters usually have enormous eyes, like *Garfield*.

If you examine a handful of comic strips, you will see some common expressions. Large, open eyes with a small dot in the center can indicate surprise. Half-lidded eyes can evoke anger. Eyes are rolled upward to express disbelief. Mouths are smiling or straight or downturned or sometimes half-up or half-down. A straight mouth is used to display boredom or disinterest. A downturned mouth is obviously sad. But combine that with wide-open saucer eyes, and it becomes horrified and possibly grossed out.

I've even seen wiggly-line mouths that give the appearance of being disconcerted. Eyebrows are the easiest of all. They're mostly horizontal for normal, angled upward at the center for questioning or puzzled, tilted downward at the center for angry.

If you wish, get some additional tracing paper and play with these expression indicators over your original face. Sometimes, when I am drawing *JumpStart*, I will spend enormous amounts of time considering various eye and mouth expressions to enhance a gag. This doesn't mean that big, broad expressions are necessarily funnier. Humor is not that simple. Sometimes a very understated expression on a character's face can make the gag funnier.

I recommend practicing whatever you enjoy on a regular basis. Drawing

This comic strip has a wide range of expressions on the characters' faces, and may even elicit a surprising emotion from the reader: fear! Not every comic is meant to get a laugh.

every day is a way of capturing a bit of your creativity for posterity, giving you a sense of immortality. It also gives you a way of self-expression that nobody can take away from you.

MY LIFE: LEARNING TO DRAW. BADLY.

When I was three, my mother gave me a book, a cool little red book. It had over one hundred options for things to be when you grow up. I checked off *artist*. At age three. Not because I was good at it, but because I just had a love for doodling, like any three-year-old, and had already been drawing pictures since I was two.

I was especially fond of Fred Flintstone. One day, I decided to draw him.

Considering my age at the time, it probably won't surprise you that Fred's eyes weren't both on his face. One was sort of outside of his nose. His legs were quite long, his large feet pointed in the wrong direction. His arms grew out of his neck, and those arms sported lots and lots of fingers. He did, however, have polka dots on his clothing, just like the Fred I saw on television.

I remember the first time I drew Fred. I couldn't wait to show my mom when she came home from work.

"Oh my goodness! You did that?" she asked, a broad smile crossing her face.

I nodded so fiercely it's surprising my head didn't fall off.

"Well you deserve a star for that," she said as she drew a star near Fred's face.

I went on to point out the tie I gave Fred (got another star for that) and hair (another star for that) and lots of other details. Mom continued to lavish me with praise and finally added a fifth and final star to my drawing.

"Robbin," she said, because even though I go by Robb now, she called me by my given name, "you did a wonderful job, and you deserve five stars!"

She then told me that I should always sign my work, just like all great artists, because my work would be worth a lot of money one day. Well, at age three, I barely knew the alphabet, and like most preschoolers, I proceeded to painstakingly scribble my name in huge letters, so much so, that once I finished the "R" the other letters had to be squeezed in up the side of the page.

My mom took that picture of Fred Flintstone and hung it up at Kleeman's, the dry cleaner where she worked.

I continued to draw many Freds over the course of my childhood, and my mom continued to praise each one of them, always telling me how gifted and talented I was.

By the time I was ten, I was writing stories to go with my drawings. I even created a small book, *Mr. Birdie the Bluebird*. As I recall, in it, the bluebird is injured, and a kid named Timmy nurses it back to health.

My mom went crazy over it. "This is a children's book unlike any other children's book," she said. She mailed it off to New York publishers to get her ten-year-old son a book deal. It went to Random House and also to Scholastic. They rejected it. I was heartbroken. How could someone else reject what my mom had raved over? How could people I didn't know, and who didn't know me, hate me so?

"Don't pay attention to those people," Mom said. "They don't understand. We gave them a chance, and they blew it! Not everyone sees what I'm seeing here, and no one sees things the way you do. You have the vision, the artist's eye."

I learned a valuable lesson from that first rejection and from my mother's reaction to it. At age ten, I realized that it was important to be persistent and not be discouraged by rejection. Years later, when I pursued syndication of my comic strips, I had a healthy perspective on it. Of course some—maybe most—of the people I sent samples to were not going to like them. That didn't matter. Those people were not the final voice, not if I was persistent.

By this time I had perfected Fred Flintstone. I couldn't draw much else, but my Fred was pretty amazing. My drawings of him were not only accurate, but I could also do them lightning fast. So much so that when the school bully decided to pick on me (yes, he had the much underappreciated decorum to inform me ahead of time that he was in the mood to beat me up!), I grabbed some paper and did a rapid sketch of Fred Flintstone. The bully liked it and asked me to do it again. I did.

At that age and in that tight-knit, row-house neighborhood (let's be honest and call it a ghetto), being able to draw anything—and especially the cartoon characters we kids watched every day on television—was powerful stuff. I was the envy of all, and my drawings became a calling card of sorts.

The bully was so impressed that he forgot all about his plan to pummel me. Instead, he asked, rather meekly, "Can I take this home?"

I signed my Fred—quickly—and told the bully that he could have it. Phew. I made an instant friend (and we're friends to this day), just by drawing. I thought this was cool. I realized then that my drawing talent could open doors, turn enemies into friends, and even keep my nose intact. My art is my armor.

In the following years, I moved on to drawing Charlie Brown and then Snoopy. Later, there were other comics I emulated, before eventually I created my own characters.

Life Lesson: Focus on what you love to do and work hard to do it well.

The old adage "practice makes perfect" is true. But it's useless if you are forced to practice something you hate. In the drawing lesson at the start of this chapter, I asked you to draw yourself as a cartoon character. Odds are that you can do better than I did with my first Fred Flintstone. You could hardly do worse. But I also asked you to play around a bit, to try different expressions. This required some persistence on your part, and persistence is a good trait to cultivate. And drawing various cartoons of yourself is fun, too.

Chapter 3

I HAVE A LOVING, SAFE HOME DURING A VIOLENT ERA

DRAWING LESSON:
Capture perspective in your drawing.

WHAT YOU WILL NEED:

- Pad of drawing paper
- Straight-edge ruler
- Writing tool (a pencil is okay, though I usually don't recommend it)

THE LESSON

Without some understanding of perspective and how to capture it in a drawing, nothing turns out looking "right." Children have an especially difficult time with perspective. A drawing of their family home will look flat. I mean *really* flat! Green grass directly under a square house with a triangle for a roof: flat. Life has depth. All a child has to do is keep on livin' to discover how much depth there is!

But how can we capture that depth in our drawings? Well, lessons on this topic can get complicated. My son recently told me it's his hardest class in art college. I will try to make it simple for you by breaking it down into three steps.

I recently went to a corporate plaza in Los Angeles, where I sat on the edge of a fountain and started sketching away. I chose the location because of its beauty and complexity. There were a lot of hard-edged geometric shapes in the plaza, and lots of organic shapes, too. Do not be intimidated by landscapes and cityscapes that appear, at first, to be complex.

In this first step, draw some guidelines as I have done in the illustration. I have lightly drawn guides, using a ruler and a pencil. I don't usually recommend pencils, but for this lesson, I will make an exception. The guides show the horizon (or vanishing point) within the scene in front of you. Objects become thinner and vanish to a point the farther away they are. As you can see from my example, I'm drawing almost no detail into the image yet. The basic shape of the fountain, and the buildings around me are hinted at, but this step is mainly capturing the slanting away of lines that converge to a point way off in the distance somewhere. That "somewhere" is usually about two-thirds from the bottom of your page, near the center—which is, incidentally, how the human eye handles perspective.

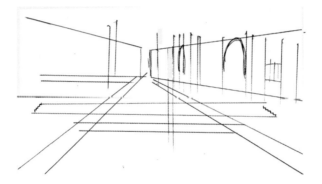

Now, in step two, we add recognizable buildings, windows, arches in the architecture, and plants. See my example and now you do the same. These are very simple shapes, but you can see the way everything must still fit within the guidelines we established in step one.

In the final step, you will add heavy shadowing to help indicate depth. Add architectural details, such as arches, doors and windows. If your scene has a fountain, as mine did, you might even add water to the fountain.

In my example I've stayed loose. The "water" appears to be scribbles, but this is not a doodle. Loose movement of the pen or pencil to make "water" creates the illusion that the water is in motion. The trees and potted plants are handled in a similar way, heavily shadowed to indicate bulk in the bushy areas and more white space in the lighter areas.

That's it. I was only at this location for a half hour or so. Try it! But remember that, as with all my lessons, the more you practice, the better you will get. Please don't be self-conscious about drawing in public places. It is a very effective way to deal with the fear factor. Just draw! If people walk by, keep drawing, without stopping to chat. You can converse, but don't lose focus. Keep going. They will usually be impressed that nothing rattles you and that you can draw and talk at the same time.

Oh, and your kid with that "flat"-looking drawing? Tell her it's terrific and tape it to the fridge.

MY LIFE: LEARNING TO GIVE.
LEARNING TO BE MY OWN MAN.

By the age of six, I was starting to pay attention to the world around me, starting to gain perspective, perhaps. And the world around me was in turmoil. It was 1968, and the Vietnam War was raging and in large part being fought by young Black men who couldn't get college deferments from the draft. At home, civil rights battles were the daily fare on television and in newspapers. Blacks—and no few sympathetic whites, too—were being beaten or having dogs set on them, even killed, in the South and in some major cities in the North. Cities were on fire, and water fountains and soda fountains were segregated. Black people (we were "colored" in those days—mostly the color of poor) were asserting their rights.

And yet, despite the turmoil, the average individual, like my mother, felt empowered somehow, able to make a difference. Black Philadelphians seemed to thrive on a cause-driven unity. There was a tremendous vibe of positivity in people. The '60s have a reputation for being turbulent, but people in my mother's social circle were positive, and on-course to make a difference.

Mom was an activist in our community, and she gave back everywhere she went. In 1965 she had met Dr. Martin Luther King Jr. and had been inspired by him, like so many others. She was involved in the neighborhood association, Citizens for Progress.

There's an old expression: "If you want something done, ask a busy person to do it." My mother was routinely called upon for lots of things. I actually thought all these jobs paid her. I thought she made our clothes because she was a talented fashion designer, not because she *had* to. I thought our only struggle had something to do with civil rights, not keeping the lights on.

In fact, Mom was given an award by the Four Chaplains Memorial Foundation. The foundation exists *"to further the cause of unity without uniformity by encouraging goodwill and cooperation among all people."*

Then Dr. Martin Luther King Jr. was killed on April 4, 1968, and the world felt like it was on fire. I cried in mourning for the first time in my life. I actually wailed while weeping and wringing my hands, like a village orphan in some documentary about a war-torn country. I felt like an innocent family member had been murdered.

Robert Kennedy was killed just two months later, on June 6. And, of course, Malcolm X had been killed three years earlier. Our heroes were dying young.

Riots and death seemed to be everywhere. I was only a child. Six years old. I was safe amid my loving family. I spent my time drawing and coloring with Judi. I didn't know it, but dark clouds were rolling in overhead, and my family's biggest storm was yet to come.

Some forms of protest are positive and forward-thinking. But others are merely small-time tribal warfare in a modern, urban setting. Despite all the civic consciousness in the neighborhood and social progress in our nation, street gangs still existed. There were three gangs in our part of West Philadelphia back in the day: The 58th Street gang, the Osage Avenue gang, and the Moon gang.

A street gang is often a substitute for kids lacking a strong family at home, a tribe of like-minded kids who offer camaraderie. My brother Billy somehow commanded respect from all of them, yet had no allegiance to any. See, with Billy, ordinary rules didn't apply, and he already had a loving, close-knit family. Kids had no interest in messing with him, or with anybody in his family. Even at age eleven, he was a remarkable little dude, and I was glad to have him on my side.

Gangs in those days rarely used guns or knives. I, of course, being a little kid, didn't gang-fight. But I remember walking to school at age five with two other kids and hearing a distant noise, the sound of many older kids shouting. The sound came closer, and I thought of a train rumbling. Then a mob appeared, two mobs actually. The Osage and Moon boys were out to settle things, or out to settle something, I never knew what. They were shouting *"Gaaang Waaar!"* and pulling off their belts. They went at one another, holding their belts by the leather ends and swinging the buckles. I could hear the strange whistling of the buckles through the air, and my friends and I took off running. I remember thinking that those kids were going to kill someone someday. I was right.

After that, I never felt the slightest desire to join a gang. My mother, in her neighborhood-activist way, later negotiated a truce between the Osages and the Moons.

I have never felt pressured to join anything. No outfits of any kind. No gang as a kid. No clique in high school. No fraternity in college. My best bet, I felt, was to be a lone wolf. Kids join gangs thinking they will get protection. I was the opposite. I got protection by just being Billy's and Judi's brother. I have always been leery of joining groups who might conspire against me. Thanks to all the praise my mother heaped on me, I'm too independent-minded to join anything. Or, perhaps, too egotistical.

Judi, in fact, pretty much took me in hand. If I wanted to go somewhere, Judi took me. Judi, four years older, was in charge of where we went. Even later, when I was ten or eleven, if I wanted to see a Bruce Lee movie, then Judi was the one to take me. And if anyone messed with me, they had to deal with my overprotective big sister.

Billy was seven years older than I am, and he viewed me as an annoying younger brother (which I was), who was often in the way (which I was). Billy had better things to do than to be bothered with me. Judi was my bodyguard, and Billy was like Don Corleone.

For a little guy, he sure loomed large.

And not just to *me*; he was larger than life to most everyone who knew him.

As kids, we were often shuffled from aunt to cousin and back while Mom worked at a dry cleaner in Wynnefield, a suburb west of West Philly that was lush and green and not at all like the ghetto where we lived. The dry cleaner, Kleeman's, was where my mom proudly hung my first attempts at drawing cartoons. She worked long hours and often stayed late to alter clothing in order to make some extra money.

Our poverty was extremely well hidden from us kids, largely because my mom was a clever woman. In spite of our circumstances, she knew how to create a fun environment. She even made utility shutoffs an adventure, telling us ghost stories by candlelight. She would wear a sheet and chase us under the kitchen table, then gobble us up with kisses!

Since money was tight and Billy liked to have cash in his pocket, he took part-time jobs carrying groceries and resetting pins at the bowling alley. To supplement his hard-earned income, Billy, who was a cutthroat bowler, also took money from grown men by hustling them at bowling. Billy was a hustler's hustler, with a charm that was disarming.

There were some horse stables to our northeast, near the Schuylkill River, and Billy was a regular at the stables. But instead of taking the horses out on the usual ride around a trail, he would show up at our apartment—in a busy ghetto—on horseback! He would have ridden the horse about four miles, some on riding trails but most on busy, paved city streets. He always took the horses back to the stables, and neither he nor the horses told the people at the stables where they had been. Billy the Kid, we called him. He was an extrovert—fearless, industrious, mischievous, generous, and wild.

Billy was self-sufficient, maybe too much so. He always had money. He "jacked" washing machines and dryers in the public Laundromats to get quarters. He gambled with older men. When I was thirteen, I was an idiot. But at that age, Billy was worldly.

My other brother, Mark, hung out with Billy as a sidekick, sort of a Tonto to Billy's Lone Ranger. Billy eventually taught Mark how to jack the Laundromat machines. My mother disapproved and made sure that I was not so influenced by my older brothers. Being so much younger, I never had any excitement—no running from the authorities with pockets full of quarters.

Billy often skipped school, stole bikes, and took off riding for the whole day. Once he even built a launching ramp for stunts. Unfortunately, he didn't build a *landing* ramp. Billy rode the stolen bike high into the air, flew over the handlebars, and landed face-first on the concrete. He knocked out all of his front teeth and sheared off half of his almond skin. For three whole days, my family forbade me to look at him for fear I'd freak out, which, eventually, I did—and I did. He had torn off part of his face; he looked like a monster. Because of his missing teeth, he had to wear dentures, like an old man. But once the healing began, Billy was back to his usual escapades, which then included chasing me around without his dentures, threatening me with the pointy vampire teeth on the sides of his mouth.

Life Lesson: Know who your personal heroes are. Know from whence you came.

While you were growing up, certain people saved your bacon. It's a good idea to tell them how grateful you are, while you still can. For me, and perhaps for you, life as a kid was one rugged event after another. When we get through our childhood difficulties and then tell about it, we often do so with an inappropriate amount of swagger. Truth is, we were protected by guardian angels: family, friends, coworkers, whomever. Like that original building in your drawing lesson, and looking so small in the distance, the people in your past may seem smaller, less important. But they're not—and never were. They helped make you what you are today. They were at one point just as large in your life as are the people standing next to you now.

When we "make it" in life, we are ever so grateful for the help we received from others who made easier our success. And, while there's nothing wrong with being grateful for good outcomes, just remember to be equally grateful for not having had to deal with the bad events, bad decisions, that your guardian angels prevented from happening!

Chapter 4

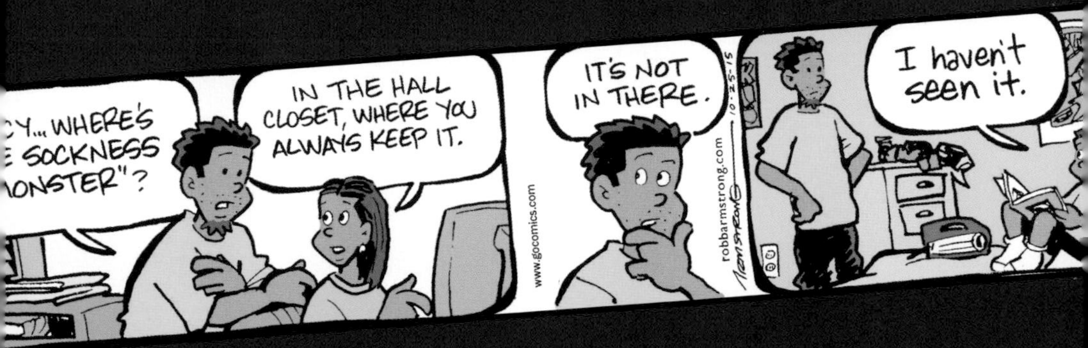

CY... WHERE'S
E SOCKNESS
MONSTER"?
IN THE HALL CLOSET, WHERE YOU ALWAYS KEEP IT.
www.gocomics.com
IT'S NOT IN THERE.
10-25-15
robbarmstrong.com
I haven't seen it.

DEATH COMES KNOCKING

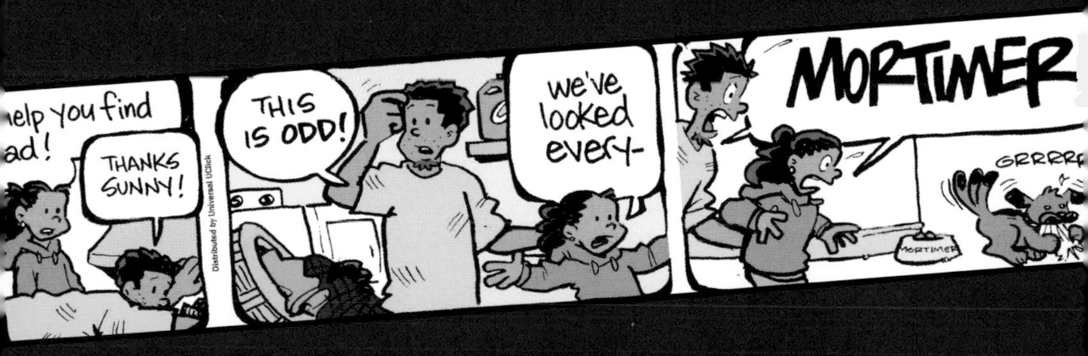

help you find
ad!
THANKS SUNNY!
Distributed by Universal UClick
THIS IS ODD!
we've looked every-
MORTIMER
GRRRR
MORTIMER

DRAWING LESSON:
Make an object bigger by adding a shadow.

This will be a two-part lesson about shadows.

WHAT YOU WILL NEED:

- Charcoal pencils. Black at least but go ahead and buy a color set. Despite the 'charcoal' name they now come in various colors.

- Pad of drawing paper

- Spray fixative, matte, not gloss. Small spray can of this will protect your charcoal and other artwork.

- Scissors

THE LESSON

For this lesson, it's valuable to draw from life, not from photographs. Life drawings, especially landscapes, should capture changing light. The shadows move. Nothing in nature is constant. You can sit on a wooded path and snap a hundred photos of it, and each image will be different.

Set up a simple still life outdoors. Be creative; don't just set out a bowl of fruit or a vase of flowers. Grab three or four things that are not typical: a lacrosse stick, an old thermos, a circular saw. Something new, something different, something unexpected.

Now, instead of drawing the objects, begin by sketching the *shadows* cast by the objects. I know that's strange to think about, but do it. The shadows will be heavy in certain areas and lighter in other areas. Try to avoid the objects themselves. Really focus on the shadows.

When your drawing is complete, spray it with the fixative. This holds the charcoal drawing in place on the paper. Otherwise the charcoal smudges. Crop into the image with scissors and trim out some of the background, as much or as little as you would like. The object here is to create an abstract work of art, a piece open to interpretation by the observer. The best abstract art pieces are often based upon real objects or experiences.

If you rearrange your still life and sketch it at a different time of the day, your work will turn out dramatically different. Shadows change constantly.

Now, let's allow a shadow to add perspective: Draw a picture of your alarm clock. (If you no longer use an alarm clock, draw something else that is three-dimensional.) Then turn on the lamp on your nightstand and shine it on the clock, casting a small shadow. Draw the clock a second time. Move the light source so it casts an even larger shadow, and draw the clock again. The clock remains the same size, but the size of the shadows makes it more prominent or less prominent.

Sometimes the shadows in our life are what we remember, long after the pain of the original event has diminished. And some events and people cast larger and darker shadows than do others.

MY LIFE: LIGHTNING STRIKES

It was a blistering-hot day on Monday, July 1, 1968. Mom was in the hospital with double pneumonia. She was extremely sick, and my sister Cheryle was keeping the family together at our Walnut Street apartment. But we all visited Mom in the hospital almost daily. On this day, Mom told Billy to ride the El into town to buy some new sneakers. She gave him some cash because she didn't want him jumping the turnstile. My brother gathered some friends to join him in the adventure.

When the train pulled up to the platform, the doors opened, and as usual, people shoved forward, anxious to board before the doors closed. Billy paid his fare and fell in just behind the crowd boarding the train. His friends, however, hopped the turnstile to hitch a free ride. The conductor saw what was happening and, in an effort to keep the train hoppers off, he quickly slammed the train doors shut. Billy, the last ticket-holder trying to board, wasn't quite in.

In the commotion, the conductor didn't notice that my brother's leg was caught in the door, leaving the rest of him balancing on the platform. The train pulled away with Billy in tow as horrified onlookers shrieked alongside the squeal of the rails. When the conductor finally stopped the train, Billy's leg was almost completely severed from his body. He paid the price for his friends' horseplay. Billy was rushed to the hospital—the same hospital where Mom was lying, sick from pneumonia—where he underwent a six-hour surgery.

He nearly survived, too. But in the end, he didn't make it; he had lost too much blood.

When Mom heard this news in her hospital bed, she sat up, turned to the side, and put her feet on the floor. Doctors, nurses, all told her to lie back down. She stood and went to take care of her oldest son. She was almost a ghost, walking the halls of the hospital, but nothing—rules, people, pneumonia—would stop Dot Armstrong when she was set on doing something. But, for once in her life, there was nothing she could do to fix things. It's frequently said that no mother should outlive her children, and I can only imagine what was going through Mom's mind at that time.

I know what was going through *my* mind. I was stunned. At age six, I hadn't personally ever known anyone who had died, and here my hero was dead. I didn't even cry; I was too confused by it all. I was not able to weep for Billy until years later. In fact, my chief memory of that time was that the apartment seemed less crowded, as, indeed, it was. Billy had been an outsized presence for a small boy, which we were reminded of in his absence.

I was too young at the time to fully register the effect of Billy's death upon my family, but I do know that it gave my mother a determination to get us out of that neighborhood. She didn't want to lose another child to the ghetto. My brother Mark, already introverted, was seriously affected, and my sisters still won't discuss Billy's death to this day. And if my father showed up for the funeral, I don't recall seeing him.

Billy's blood stayed on the tracks for a long time. Neighborhood kids used to visit the site of the accident. I was not one of them. It would be years before I'd even ride the El without adult supervision, and to this very day, every time I ride a train or subway, I think about Billy and the gruesome way he went.

My mom sued the transit system. After a bitter fight that dragged on for ten years, we were awarded about $50,000. For Billy's entire life! We suddenly had new furniture. And ownership of a row house.

We would rather have had Billy back among us, of course.

Forty years later, I was at a church service in South Philadelphia, at the Resurrection Baptist Community Church, admiring the skills of a new baritone in the choir. After the service, I sought out the singer to compliment him on his amazing voice. During our small talk, we quickly discovered that we'd both grown up in West Philly. He reflected again on my name.

"Armstrong," he said slowly. A flicker of recognition crossed his eyes. "You're Billy's brother?"

I nodded and was reminded once again about how different life was for our family after Billy's death. There was a long shadow—one that stretched for decades—attached to our very name. My surviving brother, Mark, was never the same after Billy was gone. The truth is, neither was I. It wasn't long after the accident that my mother picked all of us up and moved us out of that neighborhood, determined not to lose another child to the streets. My life was changed forever.

Life Lesson: Learn to see the beauty in the shadows.

We all face challenges. How we handle and move past those difficulties says something about not only who we are at the moment, but also who we will be in the future. We can choose whether the shadow cast by our troubled times will remain with us as a small shadow, or whether it will overtake us, always looming large. By focusing on shadows, we might see the beauty in them. I am, of course, thankful for my blessings, but it is the hardships in my life that I reflect upon and gain strength from.

Billy's short life lives on in me. And, at this point, he lives in a whole lot of other people, too. I have spoken to more than 80,000 young people in schools all across America, and whenever I do, I always tell Billy's story along with mine. We can find strength in each other's shadows, you know, because sometimes it just helps to know we're not alone. I don't care if you are the president or a plumber, we all have our shadows, dark times when we are tried and tested.

But these adversities give us our depth and challenge us to be bigger and better. It's the dark times that change us into something great, if we let them.

Like shadows that are different lengths at different times of the day, our dark times come and go at different points in our lives, too. You can't avoid them. They're part of life. But we all can take solace in knowing that eventually the sun shines on us again if we're brave enough to face another day. And in the end, it's our shadows that make us bigger.

Billy's death will always be a part of me and a part of my life, yet I could never have had the happy, successful life I have today if I had chosen to live in his shadow, or the shadow of his tragedy.

Chapter 5

WE FIND A NEW LIFE AT WYNNEFIELD

DRAWING LESSON:
Sketch your dreams.

WHAT YOU WILL NEED:

- Notepad or journal. Any sort will do.
- Pad of drawing paper
- Flair pen

THE LESSON

So far, we've focused on drawing things you see or hold while awake. But you sleep a third of your life, and your brain is processing events—especially the events of the previous day—even as you sleep. As we all know, we can remember our dreams for only a few minutes after waking. But dreams have meaning, too.

When you are untethered from your consciousness, important things cross your mind that would not float to the surface in your daily grind. In your dreams, you get a glimpse into what those things are. Sometimes dreams contain solutions. We're all familiar with the admonition to "sleep on it." In our dreams, we discard prejudices and come up with solutions our waking brain would not have brought forward.

Get into the habit of snagging these thoughts and solutions. Once you see the ideas and aspirations that float through your mind as you sleep, you get a glimpse into some unrealized potential.

Do as I do and keep a notepad and pen on your nightstand. When you wake in the morning, quickly, before you forget, jot down what you dreamed about. As soon as you are able, sketch a scene from your dream. Once you start to connect to your subconscious, you open up your mind. You start to accept imaginary concepts as real.

MY LIFE: VIOLENCE FOLLOWS US. SO DOES LOVE AND FRIENDSHIP.

Billy's death traumatized the entire family, but it especially made my mother even more determined to keep us off the streets. She promised herself that someday she'd move her family out of West Philly and away from the subway train that took her boy's life and whose distant rumble she could hear whenever she stepped outside.

Wynnefield was a Jewish suburb just north of us, so close to the ghetto and yet so different. It had big stone houses on large lots with grass and trees. Urban mansions. It's still a gorgeous place to live. My mother worked at a dry cleaner in Wynnefield, and each day, as she rode the bus from the West Philly ghetto to work, she would look up the hill toward Wynnefield and say to herself, "One day, I'm going to move up there."

For Dot Armstrong, to dream was to get her way. In 1969, a year after Billy's death, we moved to Wynnefield. Oh, we didn't move into a large stone mansion with a gardener to care for the lawn or a two-car garage for the two cars we didn't have anyway. We moved to a rented two-story duplex on Morse Street, shoulder-to-shoulder with other similar houses. But we had a house, not just an apartment.

On Walnut Street all of us kids had slept in one room. In Wynnefield, I shared a bedroom with just my brother Mark. Cheryle was almost eighteen and would soon get a job at the post office, move out and into her own apartment, and buy a Chevrolet Malibu, red with a black vinyl top. I thought this was amazing. She was the first person in the family to own a car.

But the shadow of the ghetto followed us. Shortly after we first moved to our new neighborhood, Mark was on his way home one quiet May evening after walking his girlfriend home. He was less than one hundred yards from our front door when a police car came near. As he recalls, the sudden red and blue lights were a relief to him; they illuminated the cement on that dark night.

Then Mark remembers hearing an officer yelling at him. He was hurled through the air into the back of a police van. The officers yelled racial slurs as they beat him. Mark screamed for the cops to stop and told them that he'd recently been in the hospital for his sickle cell anemia, to which one of the officers responded, "What do you want me to do? Cry for you?" Mark's facial injuries were so severe that later that night, when my mother went to find him at the police station, she walked right past him. She didn't even recognize her own son.

Mark had done nothing wrong; it was just a case of being in the wrong place at the wrong time. He was the first person to appear near the scene where an elderly Jewish man had just been robbed. My mother, who had moved her family to Wynnefield in the hope of finding a better and safer life, worked tirelessly to seek justice for Mark. She was regularly seen on local news shows speaking out against police brutality. During this time, we received death threats. I couldn't go anywhere alone.

After the attack, our lives were turned upside down. It was nothing like what we had hoped for when moving out of the 'hood and into an upscale suburb, and my family dynamic was permanently altered. Mark had already been stunned by Billy's death, which had made him a somber teenager. But this new stuff . . . this made him catatonic. Within the year, he converted to Islam and changed his name to Khabir Abdullah Matin. He shunned all things from Western civilization, and our brotherly bond was permanently affected. He and I had never been real pals; he was older and already involved with a serious girlfriend, while I was still a little kid. After his conversion, he started dressing in long robes and talked only about his religion. I have to say, looking back from the distance of time (perspective, remember), that Islam seemed a good thing for Khabir. It seemed to give him solace, comfort, and a framework for living his life.

My brother Mark, at age fifteen, in 1972 (left); as Khabir two years later (middle); and at age fifty-four, in 2011 (right).

My brother loved telling me, my family, and my friends about Islam. Though it never became something I aspired to practice, I respect Khabir for taking his religion seriously, and having reverence for God. I'm also grateful to my brother for giving me knowledge of Islam at such a young age. When the non-Islamic world seemed to be grasping for understanding of Muslims in the hysteria of post–9/11, I was aware of the difference between extremist Muslims and reverent, respectful Muslims like my brother. I knew that extremism wasn't relegated only to people practicing Islam. He spared me from becoming an anti-Islamic bigot.

Khabir and I get along well today. He's a very nice man, whom I enjoy speaking to, usually by phone, regularly. We are normal brothers, discussing family, football, married life, and the weather. Always a spiritual man, my brother will sometimes sign off our conversations with, "Just remember to follow your Ten Commandments, my brother." And I do.

I, too, was later to find myself feeling marginalized when I attended a private school. I didn't fit in at the school and, increasingly, felt I didn't fit into the Wynnefield neighborhood either. This was a weird phase in my life, during which I turned inward, seeking consolation in my own imagination.

To this day, I am able to return to this state of mind easily and comfortably. I can sit in a quiet room without television, radio, or headphones. No social media—nothing. A ringing phone will sometimes snap me out of a trance and have me wondering how long have I been sitting in that quiet space. The reward for doing this often comes in the form of original comic strips or short stories.

At the time we moved to Wynnefield, Mom still worked at the cleaners and

Dot Armstrong attending a meeting at the Philadelphia Council of Neighborhood Organizations in 1980.

continued to do tailoring on the side, often staying late at work to earn extra money. Her father had been a tailor, and she had learned the trade. But between caring for her family and working long hours at Kleeman's, Mom pitched right in to the social and political life of Wynnefield, volunteering, being active in her usual way.

Kleeman's soon regularly posted my artwork, so perhaps it could be considered the first place I was "published."

Mom opened her own tailoring shop in the storefront basement of our house and called it Dot's Boutique and Sewing Basket. Our home and the sewing store quickly became an anchor for the block.

Mom and a neighbor in front of Mom's dress shop, Dot's Boutique and Sewing Basket, in 1971.

My mom—with her independence as a small-business owner and her desire to improve the lives of everyone around her—was a perfect fit for the Wynnefield Residents Association, a place where like-minded neighborhood organizers traded ideas and tried to help make Wynnefield a promised land for the Black families flocking there from the ghetto while trying to prevent "white flight" from the old-line Jewish families that had made Wynnefield a beautiful place to live. It wasn't easy, and Wynnefield became a mostly middle-class Black enclave within two decades. Mom didn't care about that; she worked her charm on everyone, and everyone came to love her back.

Mom saw to it that we kids had fun, too. We ate off a pool table that we had in the dining room. To eat, we simply spread out a tablecloth on it. Mom also went outside to the nearest streetlamp and fastened a milk crate up on it so we could play basketball. She kept us close. It was her way of keeping us happy and safe. She organized epic block parties complete with deejays and dancing. We went to Dorney Park, a Disneyesque amusement park in Allentown, up I-476. We went to Six-Gun Territory, a Western-themed amusement park then located in Willow Grove, a suburb north of Philadelphia. We boarded a chartered bus for bowling alleys and roller-skating rinks.

We also went to church a lot, at the Tabernacle Lutheran Church near the corner of 58th and Spruce. And some summers, we went to summer camp: cabins, a lake, and Mom would come along as a camp counselor.

Every house on our street had an average of four kids, although my next-door neighbor had thirteen kids in just their one family! I went from a somewhat-isolated first-grade year to a second grade loaded with new friends. In fact, my block was so loaded with kids that it made my previous life in West Philadelphia seem isolated!

I was eleven when I developed my first real crush on a girl. Cynthia Black lived four houses away. She was light-skinned, about the same color as a roasted almond, and sassy. I loved being around her.

When Mom wasn't using the downstairs for Dot's Boutique and Sewing Basket, it became the recreation area for the family and the kids in the neighborhood. We'd unfold a Ping-Pong table and play and play. There's a scene in the movie *Forrest Gump* where Tom Hanks's character suddenly becomes an obsessed Ping-Pong champion. That was me. The only kid on the block who could beat me was Cynthia's brother, Vance, and sometimes she would follow him to watch. I could hardly see the ball because I was so distracted.

But I wasn't the only kid with a crush on Cynthia Black. Trent Stokes liked her, too, as did Robbie Roberts. Whenever Cynthia paid extra attention to any one of us, a fight would ensue. Literally. We'd fight, beat on each other. Over a girl to whom none of us could actually lay claim. Cynthia wasn't "loose" or "easy." She knew she was cute, though, and that boys wanted her. She was a bit of a tease and loved how passionately we all pursued her. I had a huge afro, and I'd dance around like Michael Jackson, singing "ABC" (*I'm gonna teach you, all about love, girl*—like I knew anything). She liked watching us as we tried to amuse her, and she also enjoyed watching us beat the daylights out of one another.

Eventually, Cynthia agreed to allow me to kiss her. Mouth closed. No tongue. She didn't want any germs.

It was a warm summer night in the summer of 1973. Nights in Wynnefield were balmy and sweet, and I remember those times vividly. A canopy of trees stretched across Morse Street from one end of the block to the other. Girls would braid the hair of us boys lucky enough to grow large afros. Mine was nearly perfect, and I was the only one among my friends with an afro that was big and round. So I'd pretend to be Jim Kelly, who played Williams in the Bruce Lee film *Enter the Dragon*, which came out that August. The dancing and kung-fu posturing eventually won Cynthia over.

Our kiss lacked passion. I was too nervous to muster up moist lips, and she was too afraid of my filthy germs to enjoy it. But it happened. Nobody could deny that it had happened. I boasted like there was no tomorrow.

Which is when I found out that Trent Stokes had also kissed Cynthia Black. I walked up to him, furious, and asked him for "a fair one."

A "fair one" was how we kids invited each other to fight, to rumble. In fact, once a kid accepted the invitation for "a fair one" and the punches began to fly, kids would sometimes inform the entire block by yelling *"Rumble!"* and a crowd of thrilled youngsters would circle the excitement.

I asked Trent if he had really kissed Cynthia, and he said, "Hell, yeah, motha—"

I said, "What did you just call me?" I didn't curse in 1973. I had a serious problem with cursing. My mother had told me never to curse, and I never did. Anything she opposed, I also opposed. Except fighting. And I had no problem asking Trent Stokes, a bigger boy with a family of three more brothers, to have "a fair one."

It was an ugly rumble. I got in my fair share, but Trent was tough, and stronger than I was. I was quick and could land punches, so he just rushed in, picked me up off the ground, and threw me face-first into someone's garden. I hit the fence around the garden, and the resulting scar on my face remained for years.

Judi eventually had to jump into the fight and deal with Trent while I ran into the house. I thought I would be permanently scarred! Cynthia lost interest in me after that because Trent had won. Plus, later on, I got beat up by Anthony Dennis in her basement when I tried to fight Anthony using moves I had seen Bruce Lee do in the movies.

Bruce Lee seemed to affect all the kids, just one of many powerful influences courtesy of city life in the '70s. Music was everywhere. My whole family had afros like The Jackson 5. *The Mod Squad* (1968-1973) was the most exciting thing I had ever seen on television. My friends and I ran up and down Morse Street recreating Mod Squad adventures. I *had* to play the role of Linc Hayes, while my friends fought over who would play the parts of Pete and Julie. My next-door neighbor Stevie hated playing Julie. We argued over whether Ali would beat Frazier. Life was lived outdoors on our tree-lined block. Days seemed to last longer then. Summers were forever.

Me, Mark, Judi, and Mom looked like "The Jackson 4" in 1973.

Movies were shown at the Capital Theater. The Capital was several miles, walking, from Morse Street and in a scary part of town called Parkside. It was the fabled ghetto, and was actually across the railroad tracks from Wynnefield. Our parents let us walk to the Capital as long as we traveled in a large group.

The Capital had started showing karate movies, and we were hooked. The Capital allowed us to watch movies all day if we wanted to. After these movies, we'd literally leap out of the theater throwing punches and flying kicks at each other. We'd taunt the ghetto Parkside kids, and they'd chase us back to Wynnefield. It was paradise. But, one Saturday was different. *Fists of Fury* was playing at the Capital. I went into a sort of trance that lasted for two years.

During that period, I began to speak in broken English like Bruce Lee and walk like Bruce Lee. I dressed in outfits like the one he wore in *Enter the Dragon*. I made a nunchaku out of a broomstick and an old chain. I carried it everywhere and practiced whipping it around my body just like Bruce Lee. More than once I nearly knocked myself unconscious. I spent a lot of time staring at myself in the mirror looking for physical indications that I had Chinese ancestry possibly linking me to Bruce Lee. I decided that I wasn't a light-skinned Black kid from Philadelphia. I was Chinese. I was the son of Bruce Lee!

Funny thing about being completely delusional: the more outrageous the beliefs are, the more likely other people are to buy into them. It wasn't long before my friends began acting weird around me, whispering that I had a black belt in the martial arts. I was the beneficiary of my own hype. I told my friends repeatedly that my hands and moves were lethal, and could not be put on public

Karate Kid. I did this self-portrait in 1974.

display. They bought it, and I rarely had to *do* any martial arts to prove any of my abilities.

I wasn't the only kid who was permanently altered by witnessing this force of nature on the movie screen. Every day, someone mimicked Lee's wailing battle cry or whacked himself in the noggin with makeshift nunchakus. A neighborhood guy calling himself Master Kake offered real kung-fu lessons. My friend Keyveat and I were his first pupils. I never missed a class, and my dedication gave birth to the rumors and speculation that I was a fearsome, black-belt martial artist who "knew stuff."

Curiosity got the best of my friends, and soon others started showing up in the class. Lynnwood, a tall skinny boy, signed up. Robbie "Huddles" Roberts showed up, too. Huddles was too silly and playful during class. I got angry and kicked him square in his chest, sending him flying backward about five feet. He slammed into an old television stored in the basement dojo, shattering the screen! Because Lynnwood and Keyveat were there to witness this shocking act of violence, my mythology grew legs and spread as if it had gone viral on today's Twitter.

The fight with Anthony Dennis in Cynthia Black's basement is a classic, and I still vividly remember it. I can laugh about it now. In fact, I once wrote it up as a screenplay called *Fists of Philly* (a takeoff of the Bruce Lee movie *Fists of Fury*).

A game of street tag that turned violent gave me the chance—whether I wanted it or not—to demonstrate my Bruce Lee moves. Anthony Dennis, my next-door neighbor, managed to catch me after an exhausting chase. He was two years older than I was. And he was *big*. He slammed me on the ground violently. I landed in a greasy oil spot some old car had left on the street. My clothes were ruined, but the embarrassment in front of my crew was what really sent me into a seething rage. My friends gasped and held their breath. They knew they were about to see some serious kung fu.

I went into my house and reemerged with a garden rake.

"*Anthony!*" I yelled.

"What's that thing in Robbin's hand?" someone said.

Smirking, Anthony came close. "What are you gonna do with a garden ra—?"

I answered his question by swinging that rake with incredible force, metal prongs first, in his direction. I caught him flush in his left calf, the metal teeth disappearing into his flesh. It felt like I'd stabbed a cantaloupe. Then came the gore. Twenty or thirty kids stared in silent horror as blood ran into Anthony's sock.

"You just stabbed me!" Anthony exclaimed.

The crowd then exploded in noise and disbelief.

"He's a kung-fu master!"

"He's crazy!"

"He better not let go of that rake!"

Anthony challenged me to a fight. I told him I needed a week to prepare. My friend Vance piped up. "Next Saturday in my basement!"

Master Kake soon had me breaking cinder blocks instead of the usual balsa wood. Keyveat was training me at his house with stretching and weight lifting, while incense and Asian candles burned around us. The buzz on Morse Street became frenetic as kids plotted on how to get inside to see the fight firsthand.

Huddles thought Anthony was doomed. I'm sure odds were being calculated in Vegas.

Rumor had it that Anthony wasn't taking this seriously, and was not training at all.

Saturday finally arrived with much fanfare. Vance only had one tiny obscured window to see into his basement, and it was booked solid. Peeking-room only.

I decided on my special outfit, the one Mom had bought me in Chinatown. It was like the black Nehru-collared suit that Bruce Lee wore in *Enter the Dragon*. Under the suit, I wore a fresh, white, fitted tank top, which I planned to dramatically shed in favor of a bare chest in the heat of battle. Baggy black cotton pants matched the Nehru jacket, and white socks with black slippers were the ultimate Bruce Lee finishing touch.

As I glided down the stairs like water (Bruce Lee was inspired by the quiet, devastating power and grace of flowing water) into the arena, followed by Keyveat, my trainer, I saw no sign of Anthony. As Keyveat massaged my shoulders to loosen me up, my corner man speculated that fear had gotten the best of Anthony. Vance quashed all that by explaining that Anthony "had to take a piss."

Anthony emerged after flushing and smirked at me. I didn't like being smirked at. He wasn't even dressed right. Just jeans and an old T-shirt. It was true. He hadn't trained!

Showtime! Vance rang a bell, and we rushed to the middle of the floor.

Anthony swiftly pummeled me into submission.

Keyveat was dumbfounded. "Do your lethal moves!"

"They're not working!" I whimpered from the dusty floor.

I owe a tremendous debt of gratitude to Anthony Dennis. I might still be confused about my ethnicity to this day if he hadn't punched and drop-kicked me back into reality. I still respect the great Bruce Lee and believe his influence instilled in me a powerful sense of self-confidence that I still draw upon. And I maintain a fitness regimen today that would make Lee proud.

Life Lesson: Dream big.

My mother is a great example of this. Mom dropped out of high school to help support her family. When she dreamed of moving us all to a better place, she worked to make that dream come true. Later, she dreamed that I would go to a fancy school and on to college—and she not only worked to make that come true, but also made me work to make that come true. She returned to night school for her degree after having five kids of her own. She was determined to get us out of the ghetto and did so. She ran her own business, and eventually she earned her master's degree from Lincoln University—whose graduates include Thurgood Marshall, first African-American justice of the US Supreme Court.

What's surprising to me, even now, is how she was able to do it without much support from others. But it is a lesson she taught me well, mostly by example. I became the youngest cartoonist to ever have his comic strip syndicated. That's because starting at age three, I had a dream to be a cartoonist. And thanks to my mother, I was never afraid to follow that dream, even when I was met with rejection.

Chapter 6

I ATTEND THE SHIPLEY SCHOOL FOR GIRLS . . . AND A FEW BOYS

DRAWING LESSON:
Try a different art.

WHAT YOU WILL NEED:

- 20x30-inch (or larger) canvas pre-stretched over a frame. Ask for this at the art supply store.

- Charcoal pencil

- Beginner's set of water-based acrylic paints. To start, just buy one basic color (not neon) "paint pot" set.

- Brushes. Various sizes of sabeline (ox hair) or camel hair high-quality brushes. You want small, medium, large tip. This is one place to not go cheap as cheap brushes tend to lose hairs that end up stuck to your painting.

- Gesso ("jesso"). Thin white paste you spread on surfaces to cover up what's beneath or just to prepare a canvas for paint. It fills in the pores of the canvas and makes colors painted on top brighter. Apply in thin layers and let dry between. Use just enough to get the job done. You want some that works with acrylics. You can buy it by the gallon but an 8-ounce jar should do for starters.

- Photo of yourself or someone else.

THE LESSON

Some cartoonists—such as Bill Watterson (*Calvin and Hobbes*), Jeff Mac-Nelly (*Shoe*), and Walt Kelly (*Pogo*)—are, or were, skilled in other media, such as painting.

As a teacher, I have met many young art students who are terrified of other media outside their comfort zone. Some who love pencil sketching will never use a paintbrush. Some fear clay, etc.

This painting exercise will help you to embrace a new form of expression. I'll use a black-and-white photo of Muhammad Ali as an example. To make it fun and easy, I want you to choose a favorite photograph of yourself or someone else. We will turn that image into a vibrant painting.

First, on your raw canvas, using a charcoal or lead pencil, begin drawing the geometric shapes of the person in your photo, as per the example shown.

Don't worry about neatness.

Once your initial image is complete, cover the image with a thin layer of gesso. Don't worry, your image, once the gesso dries, will show through a thin coat.

The absence of color will allow you to see that volume is created by treating each shape the way you'd paint a round ball: darker color in shadowed areas, no color or little color in the highlighted areas.

Everything organic, fruits, leaves, animals, us, is based upon simple geometry, solid shapes. Shine a light on a balloon or ball, you see highlights and shadows. If you can draw a balloon, you can draw a human being, everything is treated as tiny elliptical spheres, with highlights, midtones, and shadows. The great masters understood this. Don't treat a painting as a daunting "OMG" task. Look at each shape and treat it as a small elliptical shape.

When you're painting a shape, it's important to pay attention to shadows and light. I always paint the shadowed area first, working toward the lightest areas. This is the best way to create the shapes of the human form, too. Just remember that the body contains many, many of these dark-to-light shapes. Be patient as you capture each one individually.

This initial image is your "undercoat," and it need not be precise. Your image is now blocked out by black shapes, white shapes, and gray shapes, but it's still rough.

Allow this coat to dry.

On the following day, add details, like facial features. Again, find the geometric shapes, and don't rush this process.

Using acrylics, a painting could be completed in a few days. You will be surprised at how quickly you see dramatic improvement in your technique, the more you practice. Truly, the most challenging part of painting is overcoming your fear of paint. Once you dive in, your fearlessness will produce a beautiful work of art!

This is the photo I used for this exercise.

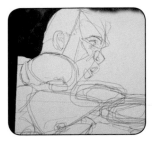

The first step was looking for the geometric shapes within the photo.

Next, I filled in shadow and light.

Take your time with facial features.

The final art packs a punch!

MY LIFE: I'M A TEENAGE BOY IN A SCHOOL FULL OF GIRLS. AND I HATE IT.

By 1974 Mom had a plan for me—her talented, gifted, genius son—and it required a change of schools.

My mom insisted that I belonged in private school. But to get in, I had to take some tests.

I failed them all.

But that didn't dampen my mother's enthusiasm for private school, or sway her belief that I was a genius. So she had me take more tests. And still more.

Thanks to my mother's powers of persuasion, when I was ready to start seventh grade, the administration at The Shipley School overlooked my miserable scores and let me in. Shipley was located across the street from Bryn Mawr College, even farther out on the Main Line—Philadelphia's old-money suburb and even today one of America's wealthiest areas—than Wynnefield. For a Black kid originally from the West Philadelphia 'hood, it may as well have been located on Mars.

The school had only recently converted from its long history as an exclusive, all-girls boarding school to a co-ed day school. There were only twelve boys and, at the time I started there in 1974, just two of us were Black. For me, it was a bizarro world.

Not only did Mom get me into Shipley, but she also got herself onto the board of directors. More amazing still, she really bonded with those folks. Frankly, she fared better than I did. It took me years to relate to anyone there.

I have to say that, through seven years at Shipley, I cannot recall anyone ever having "dissed" me because of my race. I was always treated with respect. But I was also rarely invited to other kids' homes when they had parties or gatherings at their backyard swimming pools or the like. Come Monday at school, I'd hear them discussing whatever they had done together on the weekend, and I'd be thinking, "Say what? I didn't even know you were going to do that." But it wasn't racist. Kids are thoughtless, and they want to be with kids they already know.

As I spent more time at Shipley—I attended for seven years in total—I became more accepted. I found myself sometimes visiting friends who lived in what I thought of as castles, and even once went with two school friends to spend time in a cabin on Martha's Vineyard.

Meanwhile, I was not doing well academically. As a result, seventh grade turned out to be the worst *two* years of my life. When I failed, I begged my mom to let me return to my old school. She refused. She told me I was going to go to college, like all the other Shipley kids, so I'd best get my act together.

Repeating seventh grade was humiliating. Luckily, because Shipley was so far from my Wynnefield neighborhood, I was able to successfully hide my failure from my friends on the block. That's not to say that they didn't notice something different about me. They expected me to hang with them after school. But in order to do well at Shipley (heck, in order to pass seventh grade before I turned thirty-five), I had to say good-bye to messing around with my homeboys. My mother made it clear to me: school was an all-in commitment. After school, there was lots to be done: homework, tests to study for, pop quizzes to prepare for.

But there was a fun side to being at Shipley, too. Sports!

Up until seventh grade, I had never been involved with organized athletic activities of any kind. I'd never put on a uniform, or a pair of soccer cleats. This was exciting! When they handed me a uniform in a bag, I had never seen anyone my age in my neighborhood wearing any sort of uniform. For me, this was professional sports. I loved traveling by bus and competing against other private schools. Home games were equally thrilling. Fortunately, I had grown up playing lots of street basketball and football. Dodging cars while throwing a football made me athletic enough to really stand out at Shipley. In my senior year, I was the basketball team captain and ended my tenure with an MVP trophy.

The Shipley soccer team was the first organized sports activity I'd ever been part of. This represents the entire male population of Shipley at the time (which is today mostly male). On the left is Jim Staples, on the right, John Rainey.

The male athletic program was being formed in 1974, just as I arrived. There wasn't even a boys' locker room in those early years, and so we converted the upper floor of Brownell House—a former girls' boarding dorm—into our locker room. It had no heat and no dependable hot water.

The coaches, John Rainey and Jim Staples, were charged with training a ragtag bunch of "Bad News Bears" into a respectable team that could compete with well-established rivals along Philadelphia's Main Line in soccer, tennis, and basketball. We didn't have the numbers necessary for a football program. These impressive men—who became father figures to me—were up to the task, even though they weren't given much raw material.

Sports, I quickly learned, required an entirely different form of discipline. I had to function as part of a team. Although I had physical skills, I didn't take instruction well, and becoming a team player wasn't easy for me.

I got benched a lot for failing to follow directions on the field. The coaches were strict. "Robbin, why did you do that?" I might hear. Or, "Robbin, why didn't you do what I told you?" This was often followed by, "Robbin, you're out of the game for this quarter."

Mr. Rainey once arranged for a father-and-son basketball tournament to be played at the school on a weekend. I was a good basketball player, and he certainly wanted me to be there. He even figured out how I would get to the school on a weekend, when some of the bus lines were not running. He had put a lot of thought into accommodating me. But I was still not happy. A few days before the game, he found me sitting with my back to a wall, looking sorrowful.

"What's the problem, Armstrong?" he asked.

I looked up at him. "I don't *have* a father," I blurted out. I was blubbering by then. It was coming out at last. All those years I had told myself that I didn't care—that Mom's love and that of my brothers and sisters was enough—came out. I had been forced, by Mr. Rainey's well-intentioned plan for a father-son game, to confront this fact, this hole in my life.

As I sobbed, Mr. Rainey looked down at me. "Robbin," he said, "I'll be your father."

And so he was, in more ways than simply playing in a basketball game. Coach Rainey helped me grow up, with his kind, fatherly way of speaking and his even-handed treatment of me and of the other Black students under his care. He was concerned with our growth, our development, and not just how we played sports. He was also funny and had an even temperament, something I tried to emulate. His kind, instinctive, instant reaction—a white man "adopting" a Black kid—was something I will never forget. Over the years, I would be taken under the wings of other white families, but this was my first experience of color-blind love and respect.

Even though I wasn't the next Julius "Dr. J" Erving—then playing for the New York Nets—I was certainly the finest artist ever to grace the halls at Shipley, or so I thought. A legend in my own twelve-year-old mind. Because I could draw and had a very supportive mother, I was a cocky little kid who was filled with confidence about my talent. So, a bit like my brother Billy, I treated my childhood like, "World, here I am!" Typically, one's peers will shut down such arrogance, but whenever I sketched for my classmates and teammates, the kids always *oohed* and *ahhhed* as they admired my wizardry, which further contributed to my very high impression of myself.

But schoolwork was a different story. It was difficult for me, even art class. My teacher, Ms. Wagner, routinely gave us art homework, and without fail, I'd come back the next day with a masterpiece that bore no relationship to the assignment. The class would cheer and fawn over my work when they saw my copy of the Green Lantern, or my version of Spider-Man, or a detail-perfect copy of some Justice League superhero slaughtering a bad guy.

I thought my teacher just didn't like me when she scolded me in front of the class. "This is not what I assigned. This is nothing more than some comic-book cover!" she said one day about what was clearly the best drawing I had ever rendered. Then she ripped the paper in half and threw it into the trash. At least that's how I remember it. (Ms. Wagner says she never did that.)

During one Christmas vacation, I copied some Currier & Ives–style Christmas cards, not as any assignment. I thought they were terrific and I brought them to art class. Well, Ms. Wagner obviously thought they were horrible, just one step above velvet paintings.

"But everybody says they like them," I protested.

"Robbin," she said. "Majority rule doesn't apply here."

After that class, Ms. Wagner took me aside. "Robbin, you're good, but you're not the greatest who's ever lived," she told me. I was shaking so much I could barely hear her. From anger? Fear? Awe? I'm still not completely sure.

"Look," she said. "You *could* be a great artist. You're just copying and mimicking things that are already here. I'm asking you to discover something *new*, something only you can do. Something only you have *experienced*. By using your talent to copy other people's work, we'll never find out about *your* perspective on life and art."

Part of me still wanted to hate Ms. Wagner for humiliating me, but part of me was starting to get it. I was doing completely unimaginative, unoriginal work, and getting praised for it by my peers. It was a bad combination, and Ms. Wagner understood that well. Every emotion I ever felt, and every experience I hadn't tapped into buzzed to the surface.

That day, for the first time, I was feeling *my* art, and it was coming from the hidden, dark shadows of *my* loss and frustration, not the spotlight. Soon after, I started to do oil paintings—self-portraits, portraits of friends. I slowly began to see some real ability develop. When you do a painting, especially a portrait, the result says more about you as an artist than it does about the subject of the painting.

Paint has the ability . . . paint is divine. Paint mimics life itself. Once you have committed your imagination to canvas it takes on immortality, inspires the world at large, people outside the art world, it inspires architects, city designers, fashion designers. Paint reminds us that we can do great things. You don't need to be an artist; just looking at a painting can sometimes tell a person, "I can do great things."

There's a reason you can't put a price tag on the *Mona Lisa*. It's a gift that God has given to this world through the artist, Leonardo da Vinci. But the mission—to paint original work—is important, too, and you must never stop striving to be original. The world is counting on each of us for our originality. Innumerable people have made copies of the *Mona Lisa* and, do you know what? They have price tags. They aren't the original and they can be bought and sold like so many velvet Elvis paintings on a street corner.

What Ms. Wagner was telling me was, don't be a street-corner copycat with a pickup truck full of cheap, velvet paintings. Be original. Be myself. Show what is within me.

Ms. Wagner pushed me to always be original. In 1981, I had a totally crazy original idea: I would draw caricatures of my entire graduating class, all seventy-five of them. Here's part of the finished product, which ran in the yearbook.

Taking a break from drawing caricatures of my classmates. I was exhausted!

In my senior year I also took advantage of something schools don't do much of any more. Back then, Shipley had "mini-terms," which were opportunities for seniors to intern for a few weeks at a business. The school sent me to Signe Wilkinson, who mentored me for three weeks. She was an editorial cartoonist whose work was often featured in *The Philadelphia Inquirer* and other newspapers. She had a loft office on Rittenhouse Square, one of several tree-filled parks in downtown Philadelphia.

Signe went through her daily routine for me as I sat beside her, drawing cartoons of my own. "It's a really difficult life," she said. "I don't know why you want to do this. I run around trying to sell my stuff, and they usually say no."

Well, I was seventeen or eighteen at that time, and for fifteen of those years, all I had ever dreamed of was selling one thing to one newspaper. Working alongside Signe was the most valuable lesson because it was so real. We sat there, drawing for hours. Then we would pack up our materials and hit the streets, me tagging along behind her, while she pitched her stuff in the offices of the city's various publications.

Signe taught me to self-edit. She showed me how to do a rough sketch, to hone my work to look professional, to become expert at drawing. These were good habits that would serve me well. She taught me little things, like to avoid giving characters large "clown" feet or oversized hands. Under her guidance, I did a bunch of stuff that looked really good, and back at Shipley, I got an A for the mini-term.

And Signe Wilkinson? She went on to become the first female cartoonist to win the Pulitzer Prize.

With the internship under my belt, I was a cocky kid with a professional-looking portfolio. In early 1981, still a high school senior, I walked into the offices of the *Philadelphia Tribune*—the city's largest Black newspaper—and asked to meet the managing editor. There are certain industries in which you can stroll into the building and see someone higher up, and the newspaper business is that way.

I said, "After studying your publication, I've noticed something. You have no cartoons of any kind. None."

The managing editor nodded and said, "We're a Black newspaper, and nobody is contributing anything like that."

"Well, I'm here now," I said. "I can do comics, political, anything for you. And I'm a kid, and I'll work cheap."

I had developed a certain fearlessness about my work. If you do so, it's irresistible to anyone witnessing it. Basically, I told this guy that I was about to make his newspaper a *real* newspaper.

He thought about it for a moment. "When can you start?" He then paid me to do political cartoons for the *Philadelphia Tribune*. My first check was for $75. That may have been the best paycheck I have ever earned. It validated my long-held dream. Oh, sure, it wasn't much money, even in those days. But I held it in my hand and realized that I was no longer an amateur. I was no longer a little kid drawing bad Fred Flintstone images that my mother posted on the walls of Kleeman's Cleaners. I was good at this—so good that people paid me to do it. I was a kid in high school, and I was a professional cartoonist. I thought, "I'm on my way."

Well, sort of. There was still a long way to go.

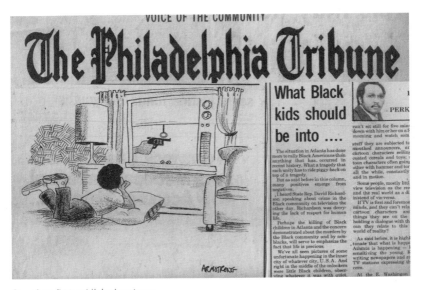

One of my first published cartoons.

I graduated from Shipley with honors. But even before graduation, I received an early-decision acceptance letter from Syracuse University.

That was the proudest day of Dot Armstrong's life.

That same day she told me she had cancer.

Life Lesson: Don't copy. Be original.

Up until seventh grade, I was comfortable with just being good at art and writing, and letting everything else go. But at Shipley, I learned that you often have to do things that you don't necessarily want to do. And by doing those things, I discovered that there was more to me than just my art and writing.

At Shipley, I met demanding teachers. The private-school education forced me out of a box in which I had been comfortable. Suddenly, I found myself memorizing Chaucer (in the original Middle English). I had to learn Latin. I had to memorize all sorts of things I had never heard of before. There was even summer homework, lists of books to be read before school started in the fall. But Shipley wasn't just about rote learning, either, or just about grades. The teachers there felt it was important to broaden their students. I suspect I was the student most in need of broadening.

I usually picked the longest books to read during the summer, trying to impress my teachers. They weren't that impressed. I think I'm still trying impress Ms. Wagner, my art teacher, to this day, and when Shipley dedicated a new building to her, I showed up to make a speech, also dedicating an original cartoon to her.

I was honored to give the commencement address at Shipley in 1996. Here, I'm sharing a laugh with Ms. Wagner, my former art teacher.

But Shipley set me apart from my old friends and, to some extent, from my family. It was more than just the physical distance I traveled to school. There was also a great intellectual, creative, social, even spiritual distance. I had to get over lots of small-mindedness to succeed at Shipley. I had to learn to be willing to try things that were challenging, things hard to do, things not done before. I already knew what I *was,* but Shipley exposed me to what I could *become.*

I had depth and dimension that I would never have otherwise discovered if I hadn't been pushed to do more. We need to be open-minded and do the things that don't appeal to us in order to truly learn and grow.

Chapter 7

WHITE FAMILIES COME TO MY RESCUE

DRAWING LESSON:
Make something out of clay.

WHAT YOU WILL NEED:

- Inexpensive modeling clay. Buy a few pounds. You can also buy a clay sculpting set but for our lessons you can get by with kitchen items. You'll also want some resealable plastic bags to keep clay in so it doesn't dry out.

- Disposable drop cloth (This may get messy.)

THE LESSON

Let's now experiment with three dimensions. There are many things around you that were made from clay before they became toys, cars, or sculptures. (Car concepts are actually modeled, full-size, in clay.)

Clay is the most forgiving of all media. Mistakes can be fixed so rapidly that they aren't considered mistakes at all. Clay is a slave to its master; it can become anything you mold it to be and puts up little resistance.

Visualize something simple to start, like a coffee cup or an ashtray. Now, before you start to mold your clay, imagine turning it into a coffee cup or an ashtray. It's an easy thing to imagine. Now think of something a bit more ambitious—like a hammer. Clay is amazing. If I asked you to draw a hammer, you might have some difficulty. Hammers don't look the way you think they look. But clay is tactile. It is made to be in your hands. So is a hammer. You can sculpt a hammer easier than you can draw a hammer. If you use tools a lot, you could probably sculpt a hammer with your eyes shut, just going by how it feels in your hand. Same for anything else you're familiar with. Clay is an art form that can also use tactile memory.

Because clay is malleable, you can "erase" the hammer and make something new. You can even make something you almost never see any-where. Make your nose. You see your entire face every day in a mirror, but how about just your nose? Try making it without a mirror—the result may surprise you. What you create is what your nose *feels* like, rather than what it looks like. Tactile memory.

Now, without destroying the first nose, sculpt another one while looking into a mirror. The two noses may look different, but they are both "correct." They are both artistic interpretations of your nose.

Picasso understood this phenomenon very well, and realized that sculpting was more liberating than painting. He wanted to enjoy that same freedom while painting, and he became famous for paintings that showed the free interpretations usually seen in sculptures.

You may choose to allow some of your sculptures to dry and harden. If you decide against that, keep your works-in-progress in a plastic bag, which should prevent hardening.

MY LIFE: ON THE DOORSTEP TO ADULTHOOD, DEATH COMES CALLING ONCE MORE. AND THEN ANGELS APPEAR TO EASE THE BURDEN.

My mom was always my biggest fan and supporter. When she told me she had termi-nal cancer, I made her promise that she'd never give up, that she'd keep fighting to stay with us. She agreed, and asked me to make her a promise as well. "Even when I'm not around," she said, "don't you ever give up on your dream of be-coming a cartoonist."

I promised. Maybe I was just humoring her, not really believing there could ever be a world without Dot Armstrong and that she would get better. Maybe I was just too stunned to react, much as I had been after Billy's sudden death.

This was not sudden, though. Dot Armstrong fought with her usual all-out determination. But in those days, few people survived a cancer diagnosis. She was not to be one of them. In the meantime, my life was going forward, and it was time for yet another major shift of scene.

Although my mother earned her master's degree shortly before her death, I was the first of her children to go to college. Mom made it to the Greyhound bus station to see me off to Syracuse. To this day, I'm thankful she was able to send me out into the world. She was terribly sick by then, and walking was difficult since her bones were frail from the multiple myeloma. But she was determined to put me on that bus. When I waved good-bye, I didn't know that I'd never see her again. If I'd known, I wonder what I might have said or done differently. Hugged her harder? Held onto her longer? Would I have climbed onto the bus at all?

I was just a few months into my freshman year—November 21, 1981—when she died. I was nineteen years old. She had been just forty-nine.

Dot Armstrong was a well-known community activist, and not one, but two newspapers ran stories about her ongoing battle against cancer and then her inevitable death.

"I love working in the community because there are so many positive struggles going on," she had said in one interview. "There was a level of energy that I found rewarding. At times, even though I was sick and couldn't get out of bed, I still wanted to be a part of the development in the community."

She added, "I have put my faith in God. I'm not trembling because of what has happened to me. My hands remain steady. I am at peace with myself because of my faith."

I was away at school, of course. And Cheryle had moved away, too. Khabir and Judi, and some of Dot's friends and relatives—aunts of mine—took care of her. She did not want me to know how sick she was; she thought I needed to concentrate on my studies.

We four kids wrote a farewell letter that one newspaper was kind enough to print:

> *Mom, we will always remember the love you gave us and the respect you taught us to have for ourselves and others. We all love you so very much and know that you will always be by our side, and we know that God will take care of you and us.*

> *The rare qualities of a true and dedicated person will be felt and remembered of Dorothy Armstrong. Though we won't have the physical contact, her concern and feelings and contributions, to all concerned will be carried forth and forever cherished.*

> *In her person we found hope, dignity, love and laughter. She gave you hope through her determination. Love in the concern for her neighbors. Dignity in her strength towards the tribulations of life. And laughter to inspire others.*

> *A peace, quiet and rest are the most deserved of one who asked nothing from anyone and who gave all she had because she was grateful for every day of her life and the accomplishments for which she sought.*

> *We will not weep for her, but thank God she was a part of our lives.*

June 1981, my graduation from Shipley. Mom was its first Black trustee and attended my graduation in her cap and gown from Lincoln University, where she had earned her master's degree one month prior.

I wept anyway. At her funeral, I was completely out of control, sobbing and yelling, making one very nasty scene. Only later did I realize that I was actually weeping for *two* people. Shaken out of my childhood by Dot's death, I was also weeping for my brother, Billy, who would forever remain a child. I hadn't wept when Billy died, but I wept for him at the gravesite of our mother.

My entire world seemed to be falling apart. Part of my hysteria was also fear for myself. All the polished, cultured, educated veneer that The Shipley School had layered onto me over the past seven years evaporated. Suddenly I was back to being a skinny, penniless street kid from a West Philly ghetto. How was I going to stay in college? I wasn't exactly left an inheritance. I thought that my mother's death meant that my life was over, too.

But even in death, Mom was watching over me. She had befriended wealthy Shipley parents. They approached me at her funeral.

One man, a white man, whom I had never seen before, introduced himself as Isaac Clothier, my mother's close friend from the Shipley school board. (Mom had gone down in school history as its first African-American trustee. As an adult, I would follow her, being appointed in 1996.) Isaac and his wife, Barbara, were very Republican, blue-blooded, and very religious. Isaac Clothier told me to calm down; he said that he'd promised my mom that he'd keep an eye on me. "And I will," he said.

But on that funeral morning, all I saw was a rich white man I didn't know, and despite all those years at Shipley, I was still just a little kid from the ghetto. Could I believe him? Trust him?

Mary Hurtig was Mom's socially minded, outspoken Jewish friend. Mary had been just a voice on the phone, until my mother's funeral. Then—poof!—there she was in living color. Mary was vivacious, exuberant . . . and she had a plan.

Mary Hurtig and Isaac "Quartie" Clothier at a fund-raiser in Mary's house in 1981. This was the day the two families met for the first time.

"I'm holding an enormous fund-raiser at my home, and you are the guest of honor!" Mary told me, just after my mother's death.

Mary reached out to my mom's friends and associates. She told them that Dot's son, Robbin, was now in college and facing desperate circumstances.

"Come meet him," she said, "and write a check."

This was Mary's way. Direct. Emotional. Persuasive. She quickly became my new Jewish mother.

Mary Hurtig had met my mother when both served on the Wynnefield Residents Association. Wynnefield had been Irish before becoming Jewish. Mary's husband was a neurologist, and they had moved there in 1970.

Mom was very politically active, and so was Mary. Neighborhood organizations and politics brought them together. When Mom died, Mary Hurtig decided to rally the neighborhood. She also called the Clothiers.

Mary Hurtig organized a fund-raising event to give my freshman year a much-needed jump start. The monies collected at the benefit dinner went into a fund to help get me through college. Her husband, Dr. Howard Hurtig, treated me like a son. Howard insisted that I never call him "Doctor Hurtig" or "Mister Hurtig." He liked it informal and treated me with respect. For special occasions, such as birthdays for his wife or retirement dinners for colleagues, he would hire me to draw up caricatures or custom greeting cards and posters. He would pay whatever fee I came up with. He invited me to professional basketball games at the Spectrum, the former home of the Philadelphia 76ers. He was always smooth and calm.

The Clothiers and the Hurtigs reshaped me and my worldview. The Hurtigs gave me an appreciation for ethnic arts: for example, Philadanco was a Black dance company, and birthday gifts were often tickets to a show.

The Clothiers were also supporters of the arts. I would see a Broadway show with them or join them at the Academy of Music on Philadelphia's Avenue of the Arts.

I could talk about any subject, no matter how sensitive, with these generous families. It was a fascinating experience because the Clothiers were right-wing and the Hurtigs very liberal. I found my own beliefs to be somewhere in the middle, a bit of both. I still give a respectful ear to any intelligent person, regardless of his or her politics.

Even my idea of "family" is broad and inclusive, without regard for skin color. I simply believe that "family" is who treats you like family. It's a love thing, not a race thing.

Mary and Howard Hurtig and Isaac and Barbara Clothier also took me out for dinners, invited me into their homes for Christmas. (Even though the Hurtigs are Jews they said, "We're going to do Christmas for you." They were truly freethinking people, ultra liberal.) From these experiences, I learned about the importance of family rituals. I remember eating my first lobster dinner at Bookbinders, a family-owned seafood restaurant in downtown Philadelphia. Bookbinders was exclusive. Often I was the only Black person in the place. This broke me out of the habit of eating only in places that seemed "Black enough." I am still taken aback today by my Black friends who shift uncomfortably in their seats in restaurants that cater to an upscale white clientele.

Much of my success today can be directly traced back to this generosity. The Clothiers and Hurtigs didn't just focus on "grooming" me. They listened to me. I learned that whites are often eager to learn from Blacks—and vice versa. The key is to remove the fear that thrives on ignorance.

Barbara Clothier taught me to be more punctual to appointments, and to write thank-you notes. From these kind people I gained a depth, a well-roundedness that serves me well today as a professional cartoonist, a husband, and a father. They shaped me like a sculptor shapes clay. Molded me. Helped make me what I am today.

When I came home during summer breaks, the Hurtigs gave me a key to their house. Over the summer, I drew caricatures for $5 each on Philadelphia's bustling South Street. I needed wheels to schlep my materials back and forth, so Mary and Howard gave me keys to an extra family car that belonged to their daughter. Unfortunately, I had to park the car in a bad neighborhood, and eventually, it was broken into. The $400 Blaupunkt stereo was stolen. The driver's window was shattered with a brick. I was horrified. There was no way I could pay for the damage, and I was afraid that this would be the end of the Hurtig hospitality. Instead, the Hurtigs got the window fixed, handed back the car keys, and allowed me to continue driving the car into the same crappy neighborhood.

I had never met people like the Hurtigs. Politically left-wing liberals. Utterly lacking racial bias. Surrounded by a cadre of highly astute friends in corporate and political arenas. Their power base consisted of Black, white, gay, straight, religious, and devout go-getters. And they welcomed me as part of their family.

I thought I first met Isaac Clothier and Barbara Clothier at my mother's funeral, but they say I met them many years earlier at The Shipley School, where Isaac sat as chairman of the board of trustees and Barbara was often on campus volunteering for one reason or another. Before the funeral, I only knew their last name, famous for being on department stores in the Northeast: Strawbridge & Clothier.

"My wife and I truly loved your Ma, and we promised her we'd make certain you stayed in school," Isaac told me at the funeral.

I perked up when I heard that. I thought, *Rich white people paying my way through Syracuse. Nice!*

As if reading my mind, Barbara said, "We're not going to pay your way through school."

Rich white people not paying my way through Syracuse—and reading my mind, I thought.

"But we do know a few good charities and foundations possibly offering scholarships," Isaac said.

Isaac and Barbara Clothier in 2014.

True to their word, after my mom's funeral, I found myself in meetings with men and women who looked like the Kennedys. Some took an interest in me; some did not. When one of the biggest opportunities for scholarship money presented itself, I messed it up by arriving so late that the board members had already left.

Barbara was livid. Her face was beet-red with anger and humiliation.

When I told her I was late because of the bus, she would have none of it. "Don't blame public transportation. It was because of you, Robbin!" She shook her head in disbelief. "And look at how you're dressed."

I looked down at my Reebok sneakers and my Sergio Valente designer jeans, and felt I looked pretty snazzy.

"I told you to dress up," Barbara said.

I muttered something about this being my only clean outfit.

Again, she accepted no excuses. "People don't have to help you, Robbin," she said. "The next time you are expected to be somewhere, plan your time accordingly, and show up prepared to make a good impression!"

With that, Barbara grabbed me—literally, grabbed me by the back of my neck—and threw me out of her fancy downtown office and onto the sidewalk. It was the last time I would be late for anything associated with the Clothier family.

Barbara did reconvene a meeting with that erudite foundation, and I did show up on time, in a very uncomfortable suit jacket and tie. And I was awarded a scholarship worth thousands.

I slowly acclimated to this new, different family. I never lived with the Clothiers, but I enjoyed an open-door policy at their home, much like the one I enjoyed with the Hurtigs.

Years later, I got married, and my wife and I had two kids. After returning from a family vacation to Mexico, I was exhausted and flicked on the television, figuring it would serve as background noise while I took a power nap. But before I could drift off, there was Isaac Clothier, standing before a bank of microphones, ashen, exhausted, and grief-stricken. His daughter, Melinda, had just been murdered by her estranged husband, who had taken his own life with a .38-caliber handgun. Their three young children, also intended victims, had fled to safety.

After the nineteen years of the Clothiers being there for me, I gathered up my family to be there for the Clothiers. All lives matter.

My daughter Tess, son Rex, and wife Crystal, with Mary and Howard Hurtig in March 2007. Our three families—the Hurtigs, Clothiers, and Armstrongs— often celebrated birthdays together. Barbara Clothier took this photo during one such celebration.

My wife Crystal (far right) and I joined the Hurtigs to celebrate Howard's seventy-fifth birthday at the Germantown Cricket Club on November 15, 2015. Their son, Ben, snapped the photo. His sister Leslie is next to Crystal.

Life Lesson: Accept help.

When we lose someone influential in our lives, it's hard to imagine how we can possibly go on without that love and support, without that guidance.

It helped me to remember the words of the Black poet Langston Hughes in his poem "Mother to Son": *Well, son, I'll tell you: Life for me ain't been no crystal stair. . . .*

But while it's tempting to give in to our grief, we must do our best to keep it in perspective. Remember the clock and shadow you drew for the Chapter 4 exercise? The object—the clock—was always the same size; it was the same object. But the size of the shadows made it more important or less important.

It was you who controlled its apparent size, by your proximity to it. And that's true in life, too. People, loved ones, cast large shadows in our lives.

But in time—and with some distance—we put the shadow into perspective. But the person—the person is always there, with us, inside us.

And over the course of our lives, we come into contact with many people who are different from us, or different from the way we see ourselves.

The differences might be in upbringing, ethnicity, socioeconomic status, religion, age, or sexuality. When we choose to associate with or befriend only those most like us, we miss out on meeting some interesting, colorful, and fascinating people. We also aren't challenged to open our eyes and minds to other points of view. What's more, we sacrifice an opportunity to positively influence people's opinions about whatever group we represent.

Mom—Dot Armstrong—lived her life in a world where race, religion, and economic status didn't impede her progress. What mattered to her was giving. Giving and participating. Even after her death, she loomed large, cast a long shadow, both in my own mind and in the memories of others who stepped forward to carry her child—me—just a bit farther.

Chapter 8

HECTOR HELPS ME; CHRIST FULFILLS ME

DRAWING LESSON:
Learn to sketch fast and loose.

WHAT YOU WILL NEED:

- Black Flair pen
- Pad of drawing paper
- Pad of tracing paper
- Scissors
- Clear tape

THE LESSON

This the most important art lesson in this book (and the longest, I think). The sample you see on the next page is a rough sketch of one of my daily comic strips, and as you can see, the rough sketch contains mistakes, accidents, and other scribbles. It isn't perfect. Not even close. It could never be published in a newspaper. It isn't even fit to display on my refrigerator door.

Despite its appearance, though, you are looking at the most important part of my creative process. Without this rough sketch, the final product (the *JumpStart* original) could not exist.

I am grateful for the rough sketch—so grateful, in fact, that my own corporation is called Ruff Sketch Inc.

Making a rough sketch removes the fear from the creative process. Remember, if you will, that my final product will be published in hundreds of newspapers and that millions of readers may see it. That's a lot of scrutiny!

Fear could creep in and prevent the work from being its best. But, alone at my desk, I can create the rough sketch without fear and without scrutiny.

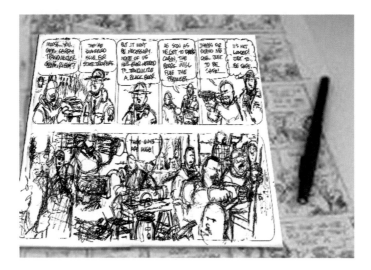

The first step in this lesson is to hold your pen in one hand and permit your mind to run freely across a blank piece of paper. This is impossible if you use a pencil. Please get a pen. Let me repeat that: *Please get a pen.* I use a black Papermate Flair pen for my roughs—as well as for my final art.

Why not a pencil? After all, it has an eraser. Well, that's the problem. A pencil comes with an eraser on it. This is probably a good thing for an accountant. But it's a useless tool for a creative person. The mere act of holding a pencil with an eraser discourages free expression. The pencil itself seems to whisper, "If you make a mark, you can always erase it if it doesn't come out looking right."

I have taught cartooning to children—ages seven to ten—who have never used a pen in their lives. They are so intimidated by the thought of mistakes that they feel "artistic" only with a pencil and eraser. As a result, most of their energy goes into removing the evidence of their expression, and the final art looks careful, stilted, and lifeless.

Let the pen hover over the page. Close your eyes and think of a story. Don't try to be funny or interesting. Just remember your own life or the events of the day.

Now retrieve a moment. Maybe it's the moment you stood in the checkout line and realized you had left home without your wallet. Maybe it's the moment you woke from a deep sleep totally disoriented, and thought you were in a different place. Whatever it is doesn't matter. That's the beauty of the rough sketch. Nothing matters. Nobody else will ever see it. This is your chance to put ink on the page with utter abandon. In doing this, you are as free and creative as anyone who has ever lived! You are Picasso, da Vinci, Schulz.

Don't draw yet. The first step of creating a rough sketch of a comic strip is coming up with the words. Using capital letters, write out your story along the top section of the blank page. The page will soon be your comic strip and the words will be enclosed in speech balloons, so plan ahead for that. Also, while doing this, remember that shortly you will be drawing characters under the words and adding boxes, the "panels" of a comic strip, so separate your story into sections like the ones you have seen in the many comic strips you have read. Don't draw the boxes yet, though. Just words. But words in groups.

When this is complete, look at the paper with the words on it. You have created the rough wording of a comic strip! The words are like clay at this point in the process. You can mold the words, remove words, cross out words, and write in new words. If things get too messy you can start over but, once I've started the drawing process, I usually just write replacement words on a slip of paper and tape that right over the original words.

No matter what you have written at the beginning, it can be improved upon to tell your story better. Any story can be made funnier just by changing the ending to make it more of a surprise. Nothing is funny without a surprise at the end.

In comics, that surprise is called a "gag." In romantic comedies, it is called a "twist"; in drama and horror, it's a "shocker," and in books and stage plays, it's the "unexpected finale." Remember this: no ending that is expected by the reader or viewer is ever considered high quality, so shape your story to conceal how it ends. Use tricks such as leading your reader down the wrong path, and then, at the last second, change the direction to the surprise. That's what produces the smile, the laugh, or a chuckle of recognition of some common truth, the recognition that says, "That's so true!" All laughter is produced this way. Nothing is funny if it lacks truth and surprise.

Once you have molded the words in a better way, you can assign words to cartoon characters. Use the cartoon of yourself you created in Chapter 2. Think of traits or qualities you want your character to have.

Now, using extremely loose geometric shapes—remember our drawing lesson about natural ovals and oblongs and other geometric shapes—place your characters near the words that come from them. You do not need to draw faces or expressions yet. Even stick figures will work just fine.

Now draw boxes around the scenes. Make the boxes big enough to contain the words and the characters. Add balloons around the words. Make the balloons roomy. Don't crowd the words, or that will make the rough too difficult to read.

At this point, your rough is a choreographed story. It is staged with the actors and their positions. You can look at this rough and see where it needs improvement.

The action should be lively and not static. In other words, no two frames should be identical. Sometimes the view is up close, and sometimes more of the background is visible. It's a rough, so make whatever adjustments you want. Nothing is engraved in stone. Words, balloons, characters, and frame sizes are adjustable right now.

Now, right on top of those geometric shapes, refine the characters. Add faces and expressions. *Stay loose!* It still doesn't matter if you make mistakes. I like to use scissors and clear tape at this stage. I will cut and move whatever needs to be changed. I will tape new words over old words.

The rough sketch should be taking shape, which will make the final sketch easy to create. Most importantly, as you read it to yourself, it should make you smile, chuckle, or nod your head in agreement.

Now, pull a piece of large tracing paper from the pad. Tape down your rough sketch, with all its scribbles and mistakes. Now your rough is ready to be turned into a final inking.

Put a piece of tracing paper on top of the rough. Now, beginning with the words, concentrate on each letter. Sloppy lettering will not work on your final inking. The secret to good lettering is patience. You want to create each letter from its own beginning to its own end. Sloppiness happens when you move on to the next letter before the previous one is fully rendered. We all know our alphabet and often get away with letterforms that are clearly incomplete. Leave nothing to chance when it comes to lettering. Make your letters crystal clear. Sloppiness, if allowed, threatens to undo all your hard work!

After your lettering is complete, draw speech balloons around the lettering. Next, add your characters, and then the outer frames. Sometimes a little bit of background art is needed. Now is when that visual information is added, but only as needed to clarify your story. If it is important, for example, that your character tell his story in a park, one or two trees in the background along with a fence is all that's needed. Don't get carried away with background art. Too much of it can muddy the communication of your comic strip. The reader's eye should be on your character or the words, not on the background fence or on the squirrel sitting on the fence. But also remember that too little background might lead to confusion about where the exchange takes place. Use your best judgment.

When complete, sign your work. It could be worth money someday.

MY LIFE: TIME TO DRAW UP A PLAN FOR SURVIVAL

Most kids—and we are all kids when we start college—have the usual adjustment problems—surrounded by strangers and no family within reach. We are suddenly thrown into a situation where we have to follow certain rules and yet we are responsible for our own time management. College life is a big adjustment for just about everyone.

But most kids don't have their only parent (and, at that time, sole financial support) die within weeks of starting school. I had lost the one person who loved me unconditionally, who took care of my every need, who encouraged me to be better than I thought I could be. Most kids, in those first weeks of college and dorm life, before they make new friends, feel alone. But they have a thread, a connection, stretching out and away, over the horizon, to their parents somewhere. Or parent. However thin, it's strong. And there.

But my mother was dead. My father had never been in my life. My brother and two sisters were living far away. I had nothing but a seemingly endless sorrow.

My eldest sister, Cheryle, took care of Mom's estate and financial and other loose ends, while Judi and Khabir helped. Khabir had also taken on much of the hard daily task of sitting by my mother as she lay dying, and tending to her. I think it matured him, and I know his Muslim faith helped him get through the experience. In the meantime, I had been hundreds of miles away in school, but they never complained about my not pitching in.

I realize now that my experience at The Shipley School had set me apart, quite literally. Even back when I attended Shipley, I was usually withdrawn on weekends, my mind more on doing homework and preparing for the coming school week than on relating to my family or friends. My friends from Morse Street noticed and sometimes groused that I was "turning white." That extreme focus made me a better student at Syracuse, but at some cost in relating to a distant family.

So, alone in my dorm room and to deal with my grief, I turned to the one thing that I knew how to do well.

Drawing.

I created a comic strip named *Hector* to deal with the grief of losing my mother. *Hector* was miserable and sarcastic. I also read and studied all of the comics in the papers for inspiration. I think I was especially inspired by the early years of Jim Davis's *Garfield*, a strip that was brilliant in its depiction of its main character, a somewhat morose and sarcastic cat. When I had some sample *Hector* strips, I decided to see if I could get them published somewhere.

Hector caught on at Syracuse University from the very moment I walked into the offices of the *Daily Orange*—the school newspaper—and pitched it to Kevin Sartoris, editor of the comics page and the art director.

Sartoris had his own very good strip in the paper, which had caught my eye because of his bold use of line and absolutely stunning lettering.

To this day, *JumpStart* has that same thing going for it—bold, confident lines and strong lettering.

Sartoris flipped through the twelve samples I walked in with, yawned, and said, "These are funny."

"Well, how come you aren't laughing?"

I spoke candidly with Sartoris because we weren't that far apart in age. I was nineteen, and he was probably twenty-one. I loved that about life at Syracuse. The whole place seemed to be run by kids.

"Your strip makes me laugh *inside*," Sartoris said. "That's why I like it. When can we start running these?"

I was ecstatic! I'd be published in the *Daily Orange*! "How about next Monday?" I blurted out.

"Monday it is," he said.

Hector ran every weekday from December 1981 until I graduated in June 1985. It was popular enough to appear in all kinds of published materials around campus, promoting bookstore sales, visiting bands, and campus activities.

Long after I graduated from Syracuse, an award was established for the best comic strip in the *Daily Orange*. It is called the Hector Award.

Hector helped me feel like a "big man on campus." I found that by dropping his name instead of mine, I could quickly make friends and attract female attention.

Many of my college friends were Black. This was new for me, in a way. Although I had a childhood with friends of my own race, my teenage years were decidedly spent figuring out my identity at Shipley—which, during my time there, was slowly evolving from an all-(white)-girls' boarding school into something more diverse. At Syracuse, I reconnected with Black people.

James West was a likeable brother from Philly. Everyone liked him. He was funnier than I was. I was extremely serious while in college. My mother's illness and death weighed on me. West could make me smile.

And when I visited Jimmy's family back in Philly, I met his father, a retired cop—great guy—who was easy to talk to, easy to listen to. When I began to develop the comic strip that would become *JumpStart*, I interviewed West's father for hours to obtain source material.

Joe, the main character in *JumpStart*, is a Philly cop loosely based upon Jimmy West's father. And Cobb—the last name of the primary characters in *JumpStart*—is taken from Cobb's Creek, the neighborhood in southwest Philadelphia where James West lived.

Mom was still with me at Syracuse, in spirit at least, and I was up to the challenge she had set for me so long ago. If I could make it at Shipley because she simply insisted and refused to give up on her dream for me, then I could make it at Syracuse, too. It was my dream. And hers. And, of course, I had her friends on my side.

Initially, it was tricky for me to embrace the Clothiers. My relationship was strained for many reasons, but partly because they wanted me to become religious. They would send me letters, some with money in the envelopes, and they usually included a Bible verse. I wanted none of it; I was having too much fun being a college kid.

I had two roommates at Syracuse. At first I roomed with Rick James, a white man with strong religious convictions. Rick and I were both majoring in advertising.

My fascination with advertising dated back to a television show I had watched as a kid. On *Bewitched*, the husband, Darrin Stephens, was an advertising art director. I always thought, "He has a very cool job." So, thinking about a career to back up my comic strip dream, I remembered Darrin Stevens, and his job, which was, as I conceived it, a marriage of art and writing.

Rick James and I spent a lot of time together in classes and at the gym. Later, he and I were joined by Eric "Rico" Hernandez, a Puerto Rican from the South Bronx. Rico went into law. For the 1983–1984 school year our unlikely trio of musketeers rented an apartment together, and they have been my good and faithful friends ever since.

Rick James was a recent convert to Christianity. He always gave me reading material, which I initially ignored. One night, in 1984, when I was bored, I read one of Rick's books, *Evidence That Demands a Verdict*, by Joslin "Josh" McDowell. It was about Jesus, but the ideas expressed in the book were nothing like I'd been exposed to in church. Once I devoured the book, I peppered Rick with questions. He thought that I needed a frame of reference for my life, a moral compass that he didn't think I'd had. He might have been right; I think my mom had been that for me, and without her, I was playing life a bit too fast and loose.

Rick was cool about it, willing to discuss it when I was interested, and willing to lay off the subject when I was not. But all this got me thinking, reflecting. I had done a number of things that I considered sinful, and they were catching up to me, weighing on me. I had become promiscuous in college, never considering the reality that unapologetic womanizing was a bad habit—even though Barbara Clothier had sometimes expressed her dismay at my behavior. I even managed to get into a fight over a girl whose jealous boyfriend kicked my butt. I was brought before the judiciary body of Syracuse and risked expulsion—over a stupid fight! My sins were catching up to me, for sure.

I realize now that this was all, in part, a reaction to my pain at being left parentless. My personal pain caused me to not feel anything for others. It was nothing evil or hostile—not that. I was just not empathetic to others' pain. I was, in many ways, a typical young man, but a bit crass, a bit dismissive of others. I came to see myself as standing outside of myself, a spectator to my life. I had grown up in a family that regularly went to church, but I came to realize that I was no longer—for want of a better word—Godly. I was no longer reverent.

One person who was there for me was Sue Lebovits. Sue was a fellow freshman, with the same major and in the same classes, and she helped me when my mother died. She was and still is a cohesive force for those in my small circle of friends. She kept us together then and has always been supportive of my career. She is another reason why I feel comfortable, whatever group I'm in—Black, white, or whatever.

In my junior year, just before Christmas, I was watching television when a cheesy, late-night PSA about adopting a starving child in Africa came on. You know the type. The commercial includes a gut-wrenching image of a poverty-stricken child, complete with flies landing on the poor kid's face.

"Please help," the ad begged.

Suddenly, my own life became vivid to me. *I was that boy!* And two families, the Hurtigs and the Clothiers, with nothing to gain for themselves, had helped me.

God had orchestrated a complex series of events using my mother and these people who were strangers to me. Strangers who went out of their way, time and again, for a kid who sometimes didn't treat them with kindness.

Once I recognized the connection, I begged God's forgiveness and accepted something bigger than me into my life. Rick and I prayed together, and then I called the Clothiers with the news that I had found Jesus Christ. We were all in tears as I asked them to forgive me for my unappreciative, and often just plain rude, behavior.

I had no idea that just days earlier, the Clothiers had concluded that they'd had quite enough of my arrogant behavior and had decided to leave me alone for good as soon as I graduated from Syracuse. So a side-benefit of my conversion was that it saved this very important relationship.

As a newly converted Christian, I gave up a lot of my college fun in favor of work. I attended Bible-study classes. There would be no more drinking and womanizing. I had not been a big drinker, but before my conversion, I had awakened in some weird places. (The weirdest place was with my head in a toilet in some frat house with kids standing around asking, "Is your friend going to be all right?" and I was thinking, *Yeah, I hope your friend is going to be all right . . . oh wait! They're talking about me!*)

I realized that I needed salvation. I had been living a life that was not going to be an asset to this world. I had not yet come even close to realizing my potential. God, I realized, wanted me to live a bigger, more useful existence. The man he wanted me to be wasn't the man I was then. My ego and my pride didn't increase me, they only shrank me.

There are many epiphanies that can help you live a better life. In my case, it was bigger than life. It was also bigger than death. My soul was no longer hanging in the balance.

My conversion and my new focus on serious matters came to the fore when I was a senior at Syracuse. I had a work-study job as a security guard at an on-campus art gallery. I also worked as an art director for the *Daily Orange*. As art director, I made sure the other cartoonists got their work in on time and that the language was clean. College students sometimes think profanity is funny. As art director I tried to raise the bar a little. I had great student cartoonists in my stable, talented guys who have gone on to great success. Bryan Buckley is now a famous movie director; and Frank Cammuso drew political cartoons for the *Post-Standard* in Syracuse before becoming a successful book author and illustrator.

For extra cash, I also worked at the printing plant where the *Daily Orange* was produced. My shift began every morning at 4 a.m. and ended whenever the final press run was done, usually around 7 a.m. Sometimes, the paper had glaring

My lifelong college friends, Sue Lebovits, Richard James, and Bryan Buckley. I am still in touch with all three. On the top is our graduation photo in 1985; on the bottom, a reunion in 2014.

missing parts: unwritten stories by writers who never handed in their work, gaps for ads that were never purchased, holes due to miscalculations about the length of a story, etc.

Not to worry.

"Tell Armstrong to draw something, *quick!*" was the all-too-familiar, panic-stricken refrain yelled over the deafening pounding of the ancient printing presses.

While "drawing something on the spot" was not in my job description, I took pride in my ability to do it. My colleagues were appreciative and brought me cup after cup of coffee, marveling at the speed at which I generated the impromptu pieces.

Whenever I'd see the *Daily Orange* around campus, I felt that I was becoming the man God meant me to be. My confidence in myself as a go-to professional was off the charts. So was my insomnia. Living on an unyielding diet of high-level responsibility, girlfriends, schoolwork, graveyard shifts, and coffee relegated sleep to sudden catnaps throughout the weekday.

But I was dedicated. And good. College students, friends, and even professors praised *Hector,* and I found myself in a league with the athletes who preened around campus. *Yeah, I'm Robbin Troy Armstrong, the guy who does* Hector *in* the *Daily Orange.*

So you can imagine my surprise when, during my senior year, I started looking for a job as a cartoonist and came up empty.

I sent copies of my work to King Features Syndicate, United Feature Syndicate, Tribune Media, and Universal Press Syndicate. All of the responses were form letters, not even stamped with a fake signature. Was I really cut out to be a nationally syndicated cartoonist, after all? Or was I just a college-paper flash in the pan? Would my dream since age three remain just a dream? Was I not going to be able to fulfill my promise to my dying mother? Was this the life, after all, that God had planned for me?

Life Lesson: Remember that just because you can't see something doesn't mean it doesn't exist.

Remember our rough sketch? It was incomplete, changed many times, new ideas overlaid on the old. It was only at the final stage—when we added the tracing paper and set out to create the final art from only the best of the earlier work—that a true picture emerged. I was like that, a rough sketch, through my life and up to my college years, when I discovered my own true picture. And just as the rough gave way to the final image, I discovered that in order to thrive, I needed to acknowledge a higher power. It was only after making room in my life for spirituality that I felt complete. Regardless of your religion or belief, it is never a bad idea to look outside yourself. Answers aren't always found within.

Chapter 9

I GET INTO THE ADVERTISING BUSINESS

Drawing Lesson:
Draw something from a new perspective.

WHAT YOU WILL NEED:

- Pad of drawing paper.

- Flair pen

THE LESSON

Remember the lesson on perspective from Chapter 3? It's time to try a new perspective by drawing a scene from above. Go to an indoor shopping mall (or any other busy scene you can view from above), and draw the activity on the first level from a position up on the second level.

When drawing movement, it is important to keep your pen in motion.

Can't do it? This is a difficult concept to visualize. Try this experiment: Don't look at the paper. Hold it in your lap. Look at the scene before you and draw without looking at the paper. You want to capture gestures. Just scribble the overall shape of it. Stay loose and scribbly. This will get you out of the habit of being obsessed with perfect marks on paper. A good gesture drawing looks like pure energy.

You can practice this trick at any time. At first, you may see only a page with scribbles. But soon you'll start to connect what your eye sees with what your fingers draw. Think of this as a variation on your clay work, where tactile memory helped you so much. You are translating—through your brain and neural pathways—your vision (the eye) to your creation (your hand) in an indirect manner.

Ignore details, and follow the action! It can be a rush to draw with this kind of abandon, just capturing gesture. A young mom tending to a crying toddler, a teenager window-shopping. Gesture-drawing from a high perch will give you a new perspective on form, motion, and your ability to capture them.

MY LIFE: GOODBYE, HECTOR. HELLO, RAT RACE.

Sadly, and to my astonishment, my college comic strip didn't make it outside of Syracuse University. It wasn't for lack of trying. I started routinely sending out samples to all the big syndicates in my junior year, but they just as routinely rejected my work.

One day, while sitting in my room discussing holiday plans with my roommate Rick, he mentioned his father's business address. I recognized it as the New York base of King Features Syndicate. I had a brainstorm; I would visit my roommate in New York and go in person to see King Features. And why not? Back when I was a kid, I'd walked into the offices of the *Philadelphia Tribune* and talked that editor into buying my work. And I wasn't just a little kid any more. I was Robb Armstrong, of *Hector* fame.

The editor at King was Bill Yates, who was also the president of King and the largest figure in the world of comic-strip syndication in those days. King Features was huge, and Bill Yates was huge as well, both professionally and physically, a mountain of a man, well over three hundred pounds.

So, just before Thanksgiving in 1983, I walked into the King Features office. It was exciting! My heart was pounding. A receptionist, a pleasant woman in her thirties, sat in a lobby with classic comics displayed on the walls: *Beetle Bailey, Blondie, Popeye,* and more.

"Hello," I said. "I'm here to see Bill Yates."

She looked at me, puzzled. "Do you have an appointment?"

"No. But Mr. Yates will definitely know who I am. Tell him Robbin Troy Armstrong is here to discuss his comic strip, *Hector.*"

She frowned. "I'm sorry. But Mr. Yates doesn't see anyone without an appointment."

Bill Yates.

"I'm here all the way from Syracuse University," I said. "It's too far to go back without seeing Bill Yates. I'll be going from here to my home in Philadelphia and then right back to school. Ask him if he has a few minutes to talk to me."

She thought about it and then spoke into her telephone. "Mr. Yates, there is a young man named Robbin Armstrong here to see you." Then she looked up and, with a hint of surprise in her voice, said, "Go on back. His office is the one on the left." And, just like that, I was in!

Yates's office was big, and he had original strips of *Hägar the Horrible* by Dik Browne on his desk. I sat on a beige sofa. Yates sat behind his desk staring at me in disbelief. "What are you doing here?" he asked.

"I'm here to discuss my work."

"What do you do?"

"*Hector.* You've seen it. I have some letters from you."

"Rejection letters."

"Right," I said.

"Well, if I rejected it, I didn't like it."

"I know, but—"

"Listen, kid,' he continued. "You can't just show up, unannounced, and meet with me."

"But here I am," I said. "I made it in here."

"Yes, that's true," he said. "But it doesn't work this way."

"I've made some improvements to *Hector* since you last saw it," I said.

I pulled out a small portfolio I was carrying and unzipped it. I was about to pull out comic strips to review with Bill Yates!

But then he said, "There's a way to do things . . . uh . . . Robbin."

"You don't want to see the improvements?"

"Not at this moment. No."

My face dropped. He could tell that I was crushed. "Listen, kid," he said, "you have a lot of guts. Not being scared is very important. We look for that."

I brightened up. Obviously he couldn't tell how scared I was.

"Leave the portfolio," he said. "I'll look at your new version of *Hector.* I promise."

Bill Yates did, indeed, look through my work, just as he had promised. A few weeks later, he returned it all to me. Rejected.

I'm not a masochist, I don't enjoy rejection. But Yates's rejection at that point was the most honest rejection I had yet received. Other rejections had come from people who didn't know me, who had never seen me, and who may not have had the authority that Bill Yates had in the comic-strip universe. But this, this was different, more real. Bill Yates had agreed to meet me. He had looked me in the eye, told me he liked my guts, and then rejected my strip.

There's what I sometimes think of as a curse on Black people, a tendency to assume that any rejection, any failure, is a result of racial bias. If some white people dismiss Blacks on the basis of skin tone, then some Blacks also assume any rejection is a result of skin tone. There are two sides of the same coin, and neither one is valid.

After I saw Bill Yates, I never slipped into the bias excuse again. He didn't have to agree to meet me. He gave me a second chance. And he still found my work wanting. I was not yet ready for syndication.

I began immediately to work on *Hector* and improve it. I realized playtime was over. Time to get real, get serious. The next person to see this, I told myself, is going to see me at my best. My work was what was on trial.

I graduated in June of 1985, and over the next two years, I sent out lots of submissions. *Hector* had graduated, too, and I was hell-bent on doing something autobiographical. So, out of college, Hector was back at home. But I needed more identity for his family. I decided his dad was a police officer. Hector was living at home, and his parents were trying to steer him to a profession.

I was rejected by everyone. This is not all that unusual in the writing world. In fact, I came to find rejection letters encouraging.

Most of the criticism had to do with the writing, not the artwork. It was not fun. Rejection hurts. But it didn't deter me. It's not necessarily terrible if you take the time to read what they say about you. (Those who say anything at all about you, that is. Many rejections are totally impersonal. But when they're not, sit up and pay attention.)

When the rejections started to actually critique my strips, in written letters, telling me that I really sucked—and exactly how—I knew I was closing in. That was great, I thought.

But after college, I had a living to earn. I had to find a job.

There were two . . . *tiers* . . . I suppose you could call it, of students in my class at Syracuse who were majoring in advertising. In my mind, a half dozen of us were top-tier and the rest were second-level. The distinction, to me, was a combination of grades, activities, imagination, and moxie—all essential to break into the cutthroat advertising world. I was top-tier.

When we graduated, the top-tier people went to major New York advertising agencies. All but me.

I applied to those agencies, too. Most of them ignored me. Finally, one agency agreed to hire me as an artist in what they called the "bull pen." I'd be one of a number of artists drawing up the concepts and storyboards sent down to us by none other than a guy who was second-tier in my class at Syracuse!

A big ego is a big target, and mine was blasted in the bull's-eye. "Pride goeth before destruction, and a haughty spirit before a fall," as Proverbs 16:18 puts it. Be that as it may, I was not about to become some Step-'n'-Fetchit for someone else, someone I knew to be not as good as I was.

Was I not given the opportunities afforded my fellow classmates because I was Black? Advertising is a profession in which people make assumptions about large demographics. Young people shop here. Women like this. Blacks believe that. It's not individual bigotry, nothing like that. In those days it was just built into the profession, into the mechanics of creating advertising campaigns. They didn't think of people as individuals, only as demographics. They didn't dislike Blacks. They thought of Blacks as a certain subset of shoppers. Perhaps they didn't think of Blacks as fellow employees.

I suffer from some typical forms of "Black neurosis." When opportunities don't come my way, I wonder if race influenced those decisions. It's not healthy. I wish I could say I never ponder such things, but I do. I had been excited about being a part of the New York City advertising agency scene, but, instead, I was offered a lesser job than was given to a less-qualified person. Maybe they just didn't like my portfolio. . . .

Thinking back on it, I realize I was arrogant about it. Were I able now to whisper into the ear of that younger Robb Armstrong, I'd have said, "Take the job. You can work your way up from that. Don't be prideful."

Instead, I put my tail between my legs and headed back to Philadelphia. Since I had no money, I moved back into the house in Wynnefield, sharing it with my sisters. I would never have that New York prestige on my résumé.

Philadelphia's advertising heyday had passed in the 1970s with the once-powerful N. W. Ayer & Son. (Remember Morton Salt's "When It Rains, It Pours"?) I ended up at a medium-size boutique agency, Richardson, Myers & Donofrio, working for a creative director named Victor Della Barba. Victor was very good to me, a true friend who looked out for me. He was a talented, colorful mentor who looked and sounded like Tony Soprano. It was a terrific experience, but within a year the agency closed its doors—though a Baltimore office stayed open until 2013.

The same day Victor told me I was let go, he got on the phone and got me hired by another agency. I put my things on a rolling credenza I had brought to the office and rolled it four city blocks down the street to my next job at Lewis Gilman and Kynett.

And so I began a successful career in advertising by bouncing from agency to

Victor Della Barba, my creative director.

This is a caricature I drew of him in 1985.

agency while trying to get my comic strip syndicated. I eventually made enough money to move out of the Wynnefield house into my own apartment and buy my first car, a 1987 Subaru.

Although the work at the ad agencies wasn't what I wanted to be doing, long-term, I took it seriously, always doing my best and working hard. With time, my portfolio grew from looking amateurish to looking professional.

Usually, I was the only Black person in the office. This pattern repeated itself so often that I began to accept it as the norm. But at Lewis, Gilman & Kynett, I eventually worked for an African-American creative director named Van King. Van said everything twice.

"That could work. Could work."

"Meetings tomorrow. Tomorrow."

"See ya workin' late! That's good. Good."

Van told me once that he said things twice on purpose, to protect himself from people misconstruing his conversations and instructions. He had a methodology and explanation for everything he said and did. He was another great mentor. A great mentor.

Under Van's leadership, I went on to create an award-winning advertising campaign. In 1988, when I won a prestigious "One Show" Silver Pencil Award, it was among my proudest achievements. As a result of that campaign—for the *Philadelphia Inquirer*'s classified ad section— I was lured away to a fancy agency in Princeton, New Jersey, and given a significant salary bump.

The campaign for which I won the Silver Pencil
Award.

I won a first-place ADDY Award for this campaign.

I was on my way, or so it seemed. I was well paid and had made a name for myself in an industry that had panache. Anyone else would have been thrilled, but I
wasn't satisfied because it wasn't *my* dream. I didn't want to create award-winning
ad campaigns; I wanted to be a cartoonist. I had promised my mom and I had
promised myself, and I wasn't going to get distracted or let go of my dream.

It took four years from the time I graduated Syracuse until *Hector* evolved
into *JumpStart*. It seemed like a lifetime, but in reality the transition happened
rather quickly.

Life Lesson: Stick with your dreams.

And if it doesn't work out the first time, try again. And definitely don't give up the first time someone tells you "no."

If I'd listened to others—or allowed rejection to stop me from pursuing my dream of becoming a cartoonist and a writer—then I wouldn't be living the dream I live today. *JumpStart* wasn't syndicated overnight. It took me a long time, lots of hard work, and, yes, lots of rejection.

When we give up on doing something because we listen to the naysayers, we don't give ourselves a chance to fail. Of course, the great irony is that, by failing, we allow ourselves to learn from our mistakes, so the next time (or the next time, or the time after that), we are in a better position to succeed. We should never allow fear—of failure, of looking silly, of anything—to stop us from following our dreams. Sometimes you have to take risks—and perhaps even fail—to get better.

Chapter 10

I TAKE THE LONG, SLOW, PAINFUL ROAD TO *JUMPSTART*

DRAWING LESSON:
Master the lost art of handwriting.

WHAT YOU WILL NEED:

- Flair pen
- Pad of lined paper. Sold in stores everywhere

THE LESSON

To be a successful comic-strip artist you have to be able to create large, legible words. Sounds obvious, and it is. But very few people actually know how to do that. Let's have a quick lesson here on how to do lettering.

Now, lettering is a discipline. We have a beautiful English alphabet, but it is rarely treated with proper respect. Sometimes our handwritten notes are virtually impossible to read. Before you begin your lettering on your family tree—that's in the next chapter—get some lined paper and simply write the entire alphabet on it. This will feel elementary at first, but each letter of our alphabet requires patience and attention to detail.

Work in all-capital letters first. On your lined paper, make each letter touch both the top and bottom lines. Leave a blank line between rows of letters.

This is how I did it. In order to get good at doing the lettering for *Jump-Start*, I went through the entire alphabet repeatedly until my letters became identical each time. Draw slowly at first. Make sure the letters are perfect representations of themselves. Your letter "A" should be so good that you could show it to an alien from a distant galaxy and say, "This is our letter

'A' on planet Earth." Your letter "B" should be a perfect "B." When poorly rendered, a "B" looks like the number 13 instead of a letter.

Be patient. Complete each action required before moving on to the next action. You will find some letters especially challenging, such as "G" and "S." Your "G" should not turn out looking like the number 6. The "S" should not look like a 5 or an 8. Your "O" *should* look like a zero, however!

Sounds easy, but the letter "O" is a good example of a letter requiring patience to execute. Make it connect all the way around. Make it round. The letter "D" has a spine; the letter "O" has no spine. No beginning, no end—a perfect circle. If executed poorly, the letter "O" may look like the letter "C."

Even if you never become a cartoonist, being a person who is good at lettering will make you stand out in a crowd. Most people simply can't letter well. As we, as a society, become more comfortable using electronic communication, the art of lettering is getting lost.

Once you have practiced (and saved samples of) all the letters of the alphabet, you're ready to go on through life with a new skill that will be useful in everything from comic strips to party invitations to thank-you notes. Your friends will say, "I love your writing," and that's a nice compliment in the days of Keyboard as King of Kommunication. LOL.

My Life: A Long and Winding Road. With a Few Side Trips.

I was working at an ad agency and had an apartment and all the material things I was supposed to have. But I also still had a burning desire to be a cartoonist. That was the special passion in my life. So I once more reinvented my comic strip.

Since I could not seem to convert *Hector* to a wider commercial success, I tried other things. I made him a wise-cracking cab driver for a time, then a struggling freelance photographer, but these ideas went nowhere.

At one point in 1987, United Feature Syndicate had suggested bringing back the dad who was a cop, but with a white partner. This is, of course, was very much like the current *JumpStart*. I worked on the idea, spending long hours sitting with Jimmy West's retired-cop father, talking and listening to him. Then I created a strip called *Cherry Top* (a nickname for police squad cars). I can't say that United Feature ever liked what I created, but their criticism became less and less severe.

Cherry Top featured an older Black cop as the main character. By then I was closing in and getting personal notes from syndicates. One thing they said was, "You're a young guy. Why write about old people?" I decided to go back to what I had done in college, write about myself, people like myself. I set *Cherry Top* aside and created *Off Duty*, a strip about a younger cop and his nurse wife. In stages, I wrote about a cop, then added his life, marriage, wife, then kids.

I was now meeting the better demographic—two young professionals at work and at home—and their respective jobs required specific and easily recognized clothing. No need to explain what a nurse does. Or a cop. They have uniforms. But I still wasn't getting offers.

Once again, I found myself wondering if racial bias was raising its ugly head. Well, this much I do know: both individual newspapers and the big syndicates had the attitude that one Black cartoonist at a time was all that a newspaper could carry. Even later, when I was finally syndicated, the syndicate had to struggle to get me into some papers. Editors wouldn't even look at the strips or content. They just shrugged and said, "We've already got a Black guy."

They actually said that to me. And they still do. I'm now on the other side of the line but now they tell other Black comic strip writers, "We've already got JumpStart, why do we need another strip about some Black family?"

I doubt that it was (or still is) intentional or overt racism. Comic strips take up a lot of "real estate" on the page, and editors make tough decisions as to what to use. But, underlying all that was the unspoken belief that white readers didn't read strips

Some of my rejection letters.

full of Black characters. One was enough to meet the "diversity" requirement, and that was that. I didn't think that was true then, and nobody thinks that's true now.

I soon became frustrated with cold-mailing samples and getting nowhere. So in 1987, I walked into the *Philadelphia Daily News*. I had met Richard Aregood, then the assistant managing editor, back when I was at Shipley, when I had interned with Signe Wilkinson. He sat me down and looked at my samples. "This work is good," he said. "But you can't make money selling one comic to one newspaper. You have to syndicate. I know a Black cartoonist who can help you." He gave me Morrie Turner's phone number.

This was a surreal moment. Turner was the first African-American to have a comic strip (he created *Wee Pals*) adapted into a television show (*Kid Power*). He was a childhood hero of mine. And I had his phone number! I went home in disbelief. I was just an art director at an ad agency, not some established cartoonist.

I immediately abused the phone number privilege by calling Morrie at 6 a.m. his time and waking him up. He was in Sacramento, and, as hard as this might be to believe, I didn't know anything about time zones. Luckily for me, he didn't hang up on me. I told him that I was trying to become a cartoonist. The only thing he said was, "Let me call you back." And he did. He knew what this meant to me; he was just that kind of guy. He asked me to send him some of my "stuff," as he called it. When he talked, he sounded like a jazz musician: "yeah, man" and "it's cool" and talk like that.

He called me back after reading my stuff. "This is hot, man. This is hot!" he said. "You don't mind if I show this around, do you?"

Mind? *Mind?* Morrie Turner thought my *Cherry Top* strip was hot. Morrie Turner wanted to "show this around." I was ecstatic.

He got results quickly. I got a call from Mark Cohen, a well-known comic-strip collector. I had actually met Mark before, through the ad agency. He liked my stuff too and invited me to Ohio, where he was putting together a syndicate for Black cartoonists.

I flew to Dayton, where we all met in a hotel and put together a plan. It was a heady experience for me, to be included in this group.

We were seven or eight Black cartoonists. I can't remember all of them now, but I recognized one or two from the comics page in *Ebony* magazine. I also recognized Buck Brown. He had created a character for *Playboy* magazine called *Granny*, X-rated and horny, really "blue" semi-porn stuff for a cartoonist. The art in that comic was stunning. Real "art." Small paintings that looked like each one took a week to complete. I had always thought Buck Brown was a white man because Granny was white. He laughed it off, saying, "Everybody thinks I'm white.

I couldn't care less. The money is green." (Robert "Buck" Brown died in 2007.)

But then my hero Morrie Turner called me some days after I returned to Phil-adelphia. "Look, man," he said. "You don't want to be part of what we're doing, man. It's better for you not to be."

"I'm getting kicked out of the group?" I said.

"Your work's not like ours," Morrie said. "It's better than ours. You should be a regular syndicated cartoonist."

With the late, great Morrie Turner, creator of *Wee Pals,* and Mark Cohen's widow, Rosie Cohen, at the Schulz Museum in Santa Rosa, California, in 2007.

This may seem like it was more rejection. But I wasn't that surprised. Or dis-appointed. It's true that I was "peacocking" around, telling everyone that I knew those famous cartoonists. I was star-struck by them. But when Morrie said that to me, I agreed.

By this time, in late 1987, I was starting to feel more confident. Even people I worked with in the advertising business were saying that I should be nationally syndicated. I was *feeling* it. It was coming. I was no longer the doe-eyed kid, and I felt ready. So much so, in fact, that on a visit back to Shipley to give a talk to the kids, I actually introduced myself by saying, "I'm soon to be a nationally syn-dicated cartoonist."

Then Mark Cohen, the collector who had first asked me to join his group, called. "You have an ability, a gift," he said. "I want to send your stuff to United Feature Syndicate." I had already sent them my samples, but I kept my mouth shut. He had more authority than I did, and so maybe they would look twice at my work.

So he did. And they did. And Sarah Gillespie, an editor for United Feature back then, called. She was not as gung-ho as Mark Cohen had been, but she worked with me. She really chopped it up. We faxed back and forth almost every day (as this was before e-mail). Eventually *Off Duty* got me a development deal. They would pay me, and I would stop sending the strip to anyone else. In six months to a year, and if they liked what they saw, they would syndicate it.

My editor, Sarah Ashman Gillespie.

I was happy to get that first check. It was the first money I'd made from drawing comics since I was a teenager doing odd drawings for the *Philadelphia Tribune*. And, just as then, the paycheck validated my dream. Now the trick was to deliver, to make United Feature decide they wanted me to continue. I set to work to do just that.

In just two or three months, they called me and asked me to find a lawyer and come to New York City. Lucky for me, Isaac Clothier was not just a surrogate father figure, but he was also a partner at a prestigious law firm in Philadelphia. I could never have afforded him under normal circumstances. Isaac came with me, and we signed a contract with United Feature Syndicate.

United Feature didn't like the name *Off Duty*, though. They wanted more emphasis on the young Black couple and less on the cop aspect. They eventually came up with the name of *JumpStart*. I asked them what it meant and was told that it didn't mean anything but that it was upbeat.

"I don't like it," I said.

"You don't have to like it. The salesmen have to like it. The newspapers have to like it. Charles Schulz didn't like *Peanuts* and always wanted to call his strip *L'il Folks*. We're the ones who came up with *Peanuts*."

Well, if they can order Charles Schulz to change his strip's name, I guess they could do the same to me, too. And over time, the name grew on me; I like it now. The strip was launched on October 2, 1989. I was still working for an ad agency, but I was planning on being rich. I was not aware of how long it would take to be accepted as a cartoonist. But at twenty-seven years old, I was, at that time, the youngest syndicated cartoonist in the country. My dream, dating from that cool little red book mom had given me twenty-four years earlier, had become a reality.

Life Lesson: Say something that hasn't already been said.

I have a hard time wearing slogans. I spent fifteen years in the advertising business, and I know how slogans are created to form a mindset that softens the consumer to complete a sale.

I won't wear an advertising slogan across my chest. I do not judge anyone who likes a Nike "Just do it" statement, but promoting a marketing agenda, essentially becoming an unpaid billboard, isn't my cup of tea.

This doesn't mean I'm opposed to "I can't breathe" or "Black lives matter" or any other pro-Black sentiment. I support it. It's my agenda as well. But I challenge you, my reader, thusly:

What do you have to say that hasn't already been said? I'm blessed to have *JumpStart*, all ten thousand-plus installments, be my contribution to the socio-political-racial-family conversation. Every day, I work hard to say something fresh and new. My words will outlive me.

So . . . what are your words?

I INTRODUCE THE COBB FAMILY AND FRIENDS

DRAWING LESSON:
Create a family tree.

WHAT YOU WILL NEED:

- Sharpie pen, black at least but if you see a set of colors, get that too. Like Flairs, this is a quick-drying brush-type but quite large.
- Foam board. Buy several in 24x36-inch size. Color doesn't matter. Don't buy the cork version, it's more fragile and it generates tiny cork dust.
- Some small labels or sticky notes (optional)

THE LESSON

Begin by doing a little research about your family. You may or may not need to use an online service to do this. A few phone calls and e-mails to older relatives would be a good start. Gather as much data as possible on your family. Old photo albums may help.

On your foam (or poster) board, draw a mighty oak tree. Don't sketch it in pencil first, just go for it! Leave plenty of room for branches, but at this point, don't draw anything other than the trunk of the tree, half as tall as the page.

Now, using the lettering skills you mastered in Chapter 10, begin writing the names on your family tree. Don't draw any branches yet. Better to see how many names are on the tree first and then draw branches accordingly. At the top, write in your oldest known patriarch and matriarch. Write the names of their children below them, and fill in all the rest of your relatives from there. If your data is incomplete, you may wish to write the names on labels or sticky notes instead of directly on the board, so that you can attach them to the board later. The important thing is that every name is clear and readable!

After you've filled in all the names you can gather, draw branches to show the connections between all the people. The beauty of a family tree is that, like a real tree, it never stops growing.

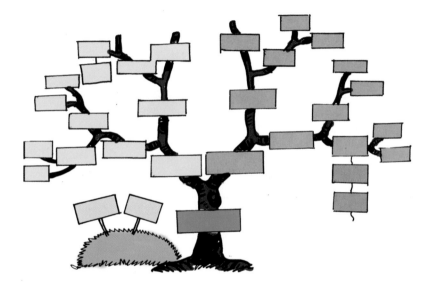

MY LIFE: CARTOON CHARACTERS AS FACETS OF THE LARGER GEMS—MYSELF, MY FAMILY, AND MY FRIENDS

Comic strips evolve, or at least *JumpStart* has. When I developed *JumpStart*, it took quite some time and several tries to get it right. *Hector* was good practice. *Cherry Top* was a first try at a cop cartoon character. *Off Duty* developed that further with a nurse and cop and its focus on younger characters. The current *JumpStart* is actually *Off Duty* renamed and improved upon.

I want my comics to show the majority of Americans (i.e. non-Black people) how a Black family operates, how they live, and how they interact with one another and with the outside world. And the fact is that they are pretty much like anyone else in America.

JumpStart offers an authentic, positive representation of middle-class African-Americans, and much of *JumpStart* is autobiographical. In fact, Joe's outgoing and upbeat mother is named Dot. Gosh, wonder where *that* came from? And his father, Frank? I suppose that, never having had a father, I'm free to invent the perfect dad to a grown son. The other characters have often been inspired by people from my own life. Here's a brief rundown of the main characters in the strip, and my motivation for creating them:

Joe: The strip is built around Joe, a sensible, well-meaning, loving man who believes in law and order and the importance of traditional values such as God, family, and a strong work ethic. But despite all these worthy attributes, Joe is in over his head. Way over! Family life is expensive and all-consuming. Birthdays, anniversaries, and big-buck holidays like Valentine's Day and Christmas seem to come around every week.

Joe just wants what every man wants: a day off to watch football and get a good night's sleep. It's not easy for an old-school guy like Joe to keep pace with four kids who are growing up in a modern world filled with things in which Joe sees no value. How do Instagram and Facebook make you a better person? And is Fantasy Football real?

Joe realizes he has love in his life, and he knows how to love in return—just not when the game is on.

Joe is the main character in *JumpStart*, and he's not quirky or weird. He isn't even funny. He's real. Joe seems genuine to my readers, and what makes him "funny" is his truthfulness. The truth, when presented in a humorous way, almost always gets a laugh or a chuckle of recognition.

Marcy: Joe's wife is an inexhaustible nurse and mother of four. Marcy wants a better life for her children than she had. This is in stark contrast to her tradition-minded husband, who wants the *same* life for his children.

There are two Marcys: "Work Marcy" is competent, reasonable, and beyond reproach. She knows just when to be funny and when to get down to business. As a cardiac nurse, she knows there is little room for error, and she lives by that. Even her superiors and the doctors she works with are in awe of her medical expertise.

"Wife Marcy" is a totally different story. She's baffled, exhausted, overworked, and snippy. Where are her car keys? The twins must have flushed them. Where is her cell phone? Check the freezer. Why is the ice-cube tray beside her bed? Joe wants to romance the more efficient "work Marcy" and talk her into coming home with him, which is why he so often visits the hospital where she works. But at home she's usually tired and cranky and doesn't want to talk to him.

Marcy is more difficult to write for because I am not a woman. To keep Marcy acting and sounding authentic, I study my wife and her friends. Often I'll pull out my cell phone and pretend to check e-mail while feverishly documenting things that women around me have said.

I have profound admiration for femininity and how different women are from men. Women who work hard remind me of my mother, who epitomized the single parent who will do whatever it takes to provide for her kids. I reflect upon her often when I am writing in the voice of Marcy.

Oh. And my apologies to Charles Schulz, who was my dear friend, but I took the name "Marcy" from a character in *Peanuts*. I even apologized over the phone to him when I did it. Schulz was very protective of his characters, justifiably so, so I was jubilant (and relieved) when he okayed my use of the name.

He not only took no offense, but later he used my last name for Franklin Armstrong, the African-American character in his strip. That happened in 1999. I remember my phone ringing and then hearing his friendly voice.

"Hey Robb,' he said. "I'm working on a DVD for the Charlie Brown gang. You know my character Franklin, right?"

"Of course. The little Black dude."

"Yes, yes. He's going to need a last name for the video. He's never had a last name. Didn't need one until now."

I had no idea where this was going. I was just thrilled to be on the other end of a "Sparky" Schulz phone call.

"Would you be okay if he's introduced as Franklin Armstrong?"

"Um . . . I'm okay with it," I stammered. "Feel free to use my last name." And just like that I became part of the *Peanuts* legacy!

It took me a dozen years to really process this unbelievable honor. In my heart, I was still just this kid in West Philly trying to draw Snoopy, and this legend among comic strip artists not only became my friend, but also believed in my ability.

Sunny: Sunny is exuberant and bright, like the sun. She loves nature, like the sun. She goes to sleep early and wakes up early, like . . . you get the idea. Sunny was "born" into the strip when her dad delivered her in the backseat of a Yugo that was stuck in traffic. This was in 1993, at the same time that my daughter, Tess, was born.

Tess is an adult now. She lives and works in San Diego. Tess was born with sickle cell, a blood disorder that can be debilitating and even fatal. Tess has had close calls but, overall, has done very well with her condition. The challenges that come with a sick or special-needs child can be a blessing in disguise. Tess helped me appreciate parenthood by making each day seem like a unique opportunity. I drew then, and continue to draw today, inspiration from Tess, who has grown into a caring, talented young woman. And Sunny, in my strip, could not have happened without Tess.

Jojo: Jojo (Joe, Junior) is based upon my son, Rex. I have always relied heavily on my real-life son to provide traits for Jojo. When Rex was a baby in a stroller, he had sticky fingers. We'd spend a few hours at the mall and then find a stroller full of unpaid items he'd filched as he was pushed down the aisles. Rex had charisma as a baby. He looked very serious most of the time, which caused people to stop and comment on how cute this "serious little baby" was.

Jojo is often depicted in the strip as running things. He's "president" of the second-grade class (even though I know second-grade classes don't have presidential elections), and he makes his friend Benny refer to him as "Boss." All this comes from Rex, who has always been a leader himself.

Rex had to endure multiple childhood surgeries for his bilateral clubfeet, for which he was bullied in school. *JumpStart*'s characters Willarbee, Percival, and Cross were inspired by the cruel classmates Rex had to deal with when he was disabled. Today, Rex is pain-free and walks, runs, skateboards, and dances with a rare appreciation and gratitude for the ordinary. And he mentors other kids facing adversity. He's a leader, after all.

The Twins: Teddy and Tommi came into my strip in 2005. I introduced them as talking, interacting fetuses. I always chuckle when I hear someone say that JumpStart is tame and not edgy. Tommi and Teddy grew body parts right in front of millions of readers! Teddy even bellowed, "Say hello to my little friend" when he grew a penis! Fact is, I get away with being edgy because nobody knows I'm being edgy. I fly under the radar, and I don't throw grenades. I use the charm of the characters to win readers over. Once won over, readers rarely take issue with anything in *JumpStart*.

Today, the twins are born, but neither can speak (yet). They communicate with each other telepathically, as they did in the womb. One innovation that began in *JumpStart* is a speech balloon that is part thought balloon. (Speech balloons are, traditionally, smooth ovals. Thought balloons are like puffy cumulus clouds. The twins' balloons are halfway in-between.)

Tommi is reserved. Teddy is boisterous and ambitious, and craves fame. A part of me loves the spotlight, too. I've acted on the Nickelodeon television show *Supah Ninjas* and in a couple of television commercials. And I really shine on stage as a public speaker. That's the Teddy in me.

The Tommi in me loves being anonymous. I can eat anywhere with my wife and friends and never get asked for an autograph unless the meal is associated with a speaking gig. At a professional engagement, though, it can become overwhelming, with me never getting to eat a bite of my food.

The Tommi in me is humble. Sometimes I even forget that I'm the guy who does *JumpStart* until it's time to do another strip.

I love writing for the twins because they give me the opportunity to speak freely about selfishness, arrogance, and other unpopular subjects in a cute, disarming way.

Frank and Dot: I use numerous models for Joe's parents. My real-life in-laws from two marriages and long-married couples, such as the Clothiers and Hurtigs, have inspired much of what happens with Frank and Dot. Whenever I am around my real-life influences, I pay close attention to what they are saying. I watch how they interact with each other.

My own mother was a terrible driver. We never owned a family car because cars cost money and because Mom was awful at driving. In my strip, Dot is "the world's scariest driver." Some readers accuse me of stealing from the police-chase shows like *Cops* on television. Actually my strip long predates those shows. In fact, *JumpStart* predates most of what you see on television today, with the exception of *The Simpsons*.

Frank is a retired cop and is the reason Joe decided to join the Philadelphia police force. Frank was more than just a good cop. He was the best ever. Nobody has a bad thing to say about his storied career. Even ex-cons whom Frank once arrested are happy to see him again, thanking him for treating them with respect, even though they were lawbreakers.

Joe wants to achieve that same elevation in his career. He discovers, though, that it's impossible to be another Frank Cobb. It's enough of a challenge just to be Joe Cobb.

In his retirement, Frank works at a Sam's Club–like store named Shop-N-Bulk, where he rose from stock clerk to head of security. When he has free time, he obsesses over his favorite comic strip, *Klondike Ike* by Vic Van Streck. This is a totally made-up strip and a totally made-up cartoonist. It's based upon nothing but my own career, and it permits me to vent about what happens to me as a nationally syndicated cartoonist.

Crunchy: Crunchy was created as a counterpoint to Joe. Joe's perky positivity needed a disgruntled curmudgeon as fertile ground for humor. Crunchy is an amalgam of many people, but mostly he is me. I'm not always in a happy mood. I look positive to outsiders and even friends, but my wife knows that I can be dark and moody. And one of the ways I deal with this is to channel my thoughts into Crunchy. Since nobody associates me with Crunchy (well, until now), I get away with saying mean things as Crunchy. He's fun to write for and keeps me in a good mood when I'm around people.

But Crunchy has become much more than that. In many ways and—somewhat to my own surprise—readers relate to Crunchy more than any other character because he's not upbeat or happy. Seeing him grimacing on a Monday morning rings true for many people. When Crunchy began dating his boss (Captain Ruiz) and eventually married her, he became the believable character that *JumpStart* was lacking. The odd pairing of Crunchy and Ruiz gave *JumpStart* fans a second couple to root for.

Crunchy is also a devoted dog owner. His beloved, spoiled Snoog-a-Boo is an übersmart canine who can do a lot more than fetch and play dead. Snoog-a-Boo can text, tweet, and post updates. Crunchy still considers Snoog-a-Boo a dumb dog because Snoog-a-Boo poops on the carpet.

The Glover family: Maureen (Marcy's mother) is a widow, husband Rick having died of a heart attack when Marcy was a teenager. Maureen has no real-life model. She is totally made up. She has been inspired by my wife, Crystal, at times, but mostly I created Maureen out of a need to give Marcy a mother. Maureen met and fell in love with Clayton, the father of Joe and Marcy's next-door neighbor. Clayton is a widower and father of twelve sons, all grown. Maureen and Clayton's union increased the cast of *JumpStart* exponentially!

Clayton's character is Bible-inspired. He's a "Jesus" character: Perfect. Beyond reproach. Never makes bad decisions. Humble, yet prosperous. After tiring of Clayton's frequent car breakdowns, his sons bought him a luxury car. Clayton gave the car to a poor man at his church.

* * *

All cartoonists face the dilemma of whether or not to age their characters. I chose not to age anyone (well, except the twins, obviously, who could not have remained fetuses forever).

Sunny and Jojo will remain children. The twins will stay small. With all respect to cartoonists who choose to age their characters in real time, I won't do it. It's bad for business. It's very difficult to market a comic strip that changes as quickly as living humans age. At the same time, I must draw inspiration from a wide variety of life's changing stages, and one way I tap into that well is by having a large cast of characters (around forty) who come from all walks of life and span generations.

And I love having so many ways to use inspiration I receive in life. I often use ideas from my life as a Christian. The Bible, just one example, is a great place to get ideas. Reflecting upon a simple commandment like "Thou shalt not covet" can result in six or seven strips. I listen to people around me, noting their actions and words. My pastor is also interesting and funny. He has no idea his sermons sometimes turn into comic strips.

Life Lesson: Don't text. Talk.

Humans are social creatures. True hermits are rare. Most of us like to be with family. We're all branches on our family trees; we have individual lives, but we're still connected. We also like to be at work with our work family. Another tree. There are other trees, too: neighbors, church, hobbies, amateur sports. The branches intertwine, tree to tree. Connections. A few decades back, it was said that the computer would make us all able to work from home. Many do today, but some people still prefer to go to an office and see their fellow workers—whom they may or may not regard as friends. Socialization.

I'm a perfect example; I can work at home, and yet I sometimes go to a friend's office, where I have my own niche and people to talk to and go to lunch with.

JumpStart, with its enormous family tree, celebrates this need for human connection. Joe has Marcy and his kids at home, and Crunchy at work. Crunchy has Ruiz. Clayton has his many sons, each with skills and foibles that give me material to work with. You get the idea.

And it's the same for each of us. We may not like everything about our friends and acquaintances, but we learn to tolerate their foibles and rely on their strengths—as they do with ours.

Chapter 12

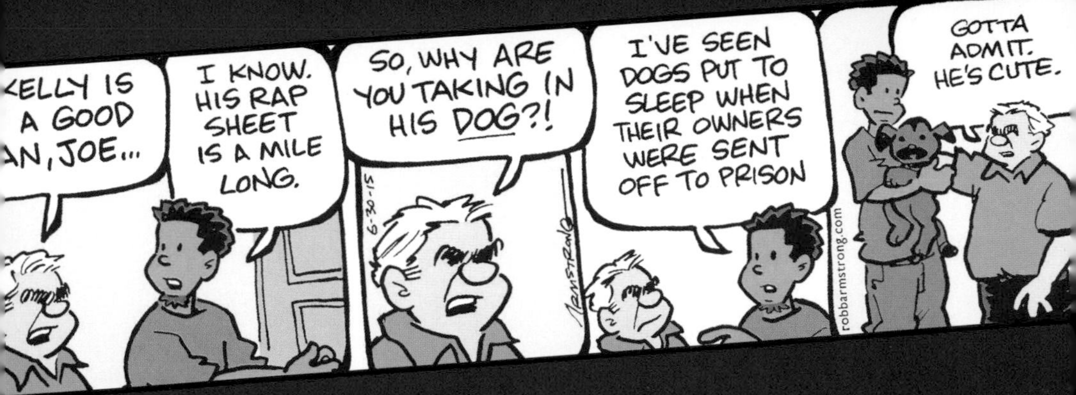
ELLY IS A GOOD AN, JOE...
I KNOW. HIS RAP SHEET IS A MILE LONG.
SO, WHY ARE YOU TAKING IN HIS DOG?!
6-30-15
ARMSTRONG
I'VE SEEN DOGS PUT TO SLEEP WHEN THEIR OWNERS WERE SENT OFF TO PRISON
robbarmstrong.com
GOTTA ADMIT. HE'S CUTE.

MY FRIENDS GO TO PRISON

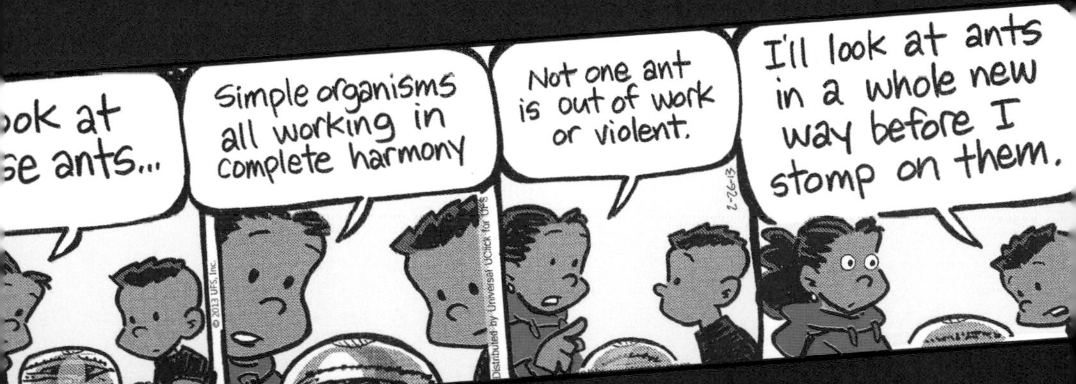
ook at se ants...
Simple organisms all working in complete harmony
© 2013 UFS, Inc.
Distributed by Universal UClick for UFS
Not one ant is out of work or violent.
2-26-13
I'll look at ants in a whole new way before I stomp on them.

DRAWING LESSON:
Learn to draw contour lines.

WHAT YOU WILL NEED:

- Pen

- Pad of paper

THE LESSON

Contour lines are used to show elevation, thickness. You have probably seen them used on some maps to show hills and valleys, a hill being shown by several concentric ovals, big oval at the bottom of the hill, small oval somewhere near the top.

Now draw your hand, but not like a kindergartener, tracing between the fingers. With your palm facing up, look at your hand and draw it.

Your hands are what sets you apart from the animals, what helps make you human. Your hands do your daily tasks, day by day, year after year, decade upon decade. They change over time, reflecting experiences they have endured. They accumulate scars, burns, calluses. They suffer; they heal; they change. They adapt. Your hands are not only not like anyone else's hands, but they're also not even like your own hands from ten years ago.

Put the tip of your pen on the paper and do not look at the paper or the pen. Don't check your progress. Just study your hand, every wrinkle and line, and translate it to the page. This is a lesson in seeing, not a lesson in drawing. When you are finished, rotate your palm so that it's facing the floor, and draw the back of your hand. When you finish, the drawings will likely look like they're of a hand that belongs to someone twenty years older than you are. Drawing each wrinkle will produce that look.

MY LIFE: LEARNING TO STAND BY FRIENDS WHO DO EVIL THINGS

Growing up in the ghetto, I did not realize or appreciate how important Mom's love and protection was for me. It came home to me during my last years in high school and through college and into working life, though, as some of my friends fell by the wayside, dead or imprisoned. There probably isn't a Black man or woman in any of a hundred big ghettos in America who hasn't lost friends to the prison system or the cemetery, but, for me, it was still a big shock when it happened.

First to go was Trent Stokes, my old adversary over the affections of eleven-year-old Cynthia Black. In 1982, when he was twenty, Trent murdered three people during a botched robbery at a restaurant where he had worked as a short-order cook. Trent and an accomplice wore ski masks. But the employees all knew his voice anyway. And when his accomplice used Trent's name, a female worker said, "Trent? Is that you?"

Trent turned to his partner in crime and said, "I told you not to use my name, you stupid motha. Now we gotta wax everybody." He ushered five of his friends, his coworkers, into the meat freezer, made them lie down, and then shot two of them, point-blank, in the backs of their heads. A mailman happened upon the scene and Trent killed him, too. He couldn't shoot the remaining employees because his gun jammed.

The Philadelphia police department back then was a controversial fraternity run by a billy-club-carrying, former cop turned mayor, Frank Rizzo. Trent feared that he would have been murdered by the cops had he surrendered to or been apprehended by them. Many young Blacks in trouble with the law had "accidents" in police custody in those days. Chuck Stone, a reporter for the *Philadelphia Daily News* and former Tuskegee Airman during World War II, routinely offered safe haven for Blacks who had run afoul of the law. They could come to his office and he would escort them to the police station to turn themselves in. So Trent turned himself in to Chuck Stone.

A jury found Trent guilty of three first-degree homicides and sentenced him to death. Three times.

Trent is now on Pennsylvania's death row. He's been there since 1985 when he was twenty-three. He was scheduled for the electric chair, but lethal injection replaced the electric chair. As a result, Trent's case became tied up in bureaucracy and death-penalty politics.

Trent and I are Facebook friends now.

I don't ask him if he feels any guilt about his crime, and he's never volunteered that information. He committed those murders at a young age, and he's doing hard time for them, still rooted in a time that passed long ago. I think that happens to people in prison. We—the rest of the world—go on, forward in time. But they remain behind those walls in a sort of suspended animation, with a worldview frozen at the moment of their terrible crimes.

Trent recently told me, in a letter, that Khabir's conversion to Islam had made a powerful impression upon him and that some lessons in faith that he learned from Khabir had served him well inside prison.

Keyveat Postell, Jr. Today he goes by "Khalil."

My best friend Keyveat did time for drug possession in the late '80s. He was, and is, an incredible person, loyal, and loving. More like a brother than a friend. Keyveat is also tough, and has more street smarts than I've ever had. The '80s were a drugged-out, crazy era. In Philadelphia, a young man with certain connections could get rich overnight, and my good friend did just that.

It is an odd thought, but I never believed Keyveat would succumb to the usual fate of young Black men dabbling in contraband. He was above that, somehow. He had the aura of invincibility around him. Keyveat had survived anything and everything thrown at him. When we were little kids, he was run over by a street-sweeping truck. I was right beside him when his bicycle was swept out from under him, and he was crushed by the truck. Obviously, it didn't kill him. Later, in an accident, he was burned in the face with a hot iron. Full recovery. He once worked as a bouncer at a nightclub. When he blocked some punk thugs from entering, they returned brandishing weapons. Keyveat was face-to-face with a hail of bullets. He got shot a whole bunch of times and even saved a young woman's life by throwing himself in front of her. I visited him in the hospital, and he had wounds all over his face and body, but made a total recovery.

By 1987, Keyveat was a Pennsylvania state trooper, his dream job. He loved the work, but the money, apparently, wasn't enough. I soon learned he was up on drug charges. For a cop facing jail time among the very people he had helped put there, this can be a death sentence. Somehow, I felt he'd beat the charges, the way he'd beaten everything else. It was not to be. Keyveat went to jail. For years.

He survived by dramatically altering his physical appearance, working out, building up, growing a beard and changing his name to Khalil. He even survived a prison riot, where he would have been killed if his identity had been discovered.

He did his time—five years—and is now living a fulfilling life. I am happy to say that my friend has completely turned his life around and is successful and quite the happy family man. His Facebook posts of his son make me grin from ear to ear!

Even my good college friend, James West, who seemed to have everything going for him when we were in school, faced some tough times. By 1991, I was working at an ad agency and making good money from it and from my cartooning. I was living my dreams. I was also living way beyond my means. I had a custom-built McMansion in Dresher, a fancy Philadelphia suburb. My comic strip was syndicated and running in sixty newspapers. I leased a 1991 Nissan Pathfinder. (Growing up, remember, I hadn't known much about cars. But my friend Keyveat had once owned a Pathfinder. Perhaps I was imitating him.) My wife and I had begun the nefarious process of accumulating debt.

One day I ran into my old college buddy James on the street. We had lost touch over the years, but I was excited to see him. "Jimmy!" I yelled. The street was filled with lunch-hour workers from all the skyscrapers in downtown Philadelphia.

"Hi Robb," he said flatly as I darted between cars to see my old friend.

He was subdued. His face lacked that magnetic light I remembered. He had recently married a woman, a Caucasian woman with two young sons, and she was pregnant with their child. Hearing this, I was so excited for him, but he was somber, blaming his mood on the pressures of an instant family.

His job was also far from a dream gig. The day I saw him, he was on duty, wearing a city-worker uniform. I happened to be familiar with it because at the ad agency I had designed some graphics promoting a Philadelphia initiative to create safer streets. Employees were put into place to pick up debris around them and act as an ad-hoc "security team," and their green uniforms looked like a hybrid between the ones worn by cops and trash collectors.

Jimmy was clearly embarrassed to be seen by me in the uniform. I told him I was glad to see him and that his job was a great one to have, with tons of benefits. He walked away, looking sad, and promised to stay in touch.

One day, about four or five months later, I answered the phone in the study of my ostentatious stucco-and-stone money pit in Dresher. It was Anthony Martin, a friend.

"Eh, Robb," he said. "This is Ant. You hear about Jimmy?" Anthony always spoke in an anxious, hurried manner. There was no way to tell whether he was about to share good news or bad; it always sounded the same, fast and furious.

"Robb, man," he said, and suddenly his speedy delivery slowed to a crawl. "Jimmy killed that girl."

"What!" I exclaimed. "What girl?"

"He shot his wife. That white girl."

James West, my old and dear college friend! I was told that he and his wife had been having terrible fights over their infant, with Jimmy often not knowing the baby's whereabouts.

During a heated argument in his car, he produced his retired father's police-issue firearm and fired a shot into her ribcage. She fell out of the car and started crawling away, gasping, "Call 911. You shot me!" Jimmy stood over her, in broad daylight, and fired another bullet into her skull, killing her. He then put the barrel of the gun into his mouth and pulled the trigger.

The suicide attempt disabled him and left him partially paralyzed.

I visited James in a maximum-security prison in 2005, about twelve years after he had been convicted of murder and sentenced to life without the possibility of parole. He seemed taller than in our college days, likely due to his weight loss. His face had been permanently altered by that self-inflicted blast, one side the familiar Jimmy I had known back at Syracuse, the other frozen in the grimace of a man in the midst of a murder/suicide.

"Watch your kids, Robb," was his greeting to me. "I'm in here with animals. Monsters. Child predators doing short bids—five years or so. They're not sorry for what they did, and they cannot wait to get out and do it again. Me, I'm never getting out, and I'm the only sane person in here."

We talked a little about my life and God. Jimmy knew I had achieved my long-standing dream. We talked about him. He had become a changed man, a positive elder statesman and spiritual leader behind the walls of the prison.

You draw advice, strength, comfort, even wisdom sometimes, from the strangest of sources. I don't know if James knows what a debt I owe to him. But here it is: Later in my life, when I faced some terrible times, when I was sometimes almost tempted to violence, I hearkened back to my friend and how he had destroyed his life as well as that of others. Even my friend Jimmy's serving as a horrible example may have—in some roundabout way—brought some good to the world. It certainly did to me.

Life Lesson: Be loyal.

We all collect scars. And we collect experience. And we change to reflect that. We can learn from our own mistakes and successes, and also from those of our friends and neighbors. And with age and experience comes the wisdom to be able to see the glimmer of good even in a person who has done unspeakable evil. There are people whom I once knew and was close to, to whom I never will speak again. And yet I am still in contact with men guilty of heinous crimes. What gives?

Loyalty. Loyalty deserves to be a protected commodity. The imprisoned men whom I happen to know are paying their debts using the days of their lives as currency. I am not here on this earth to judge them. In fact, I happen to know—because they have both told me—that they are proud to say I'm their friend.

We collect our wisdom from many sources, many people. And if Jesus can forgive the sinner but not the sin, we certainly can retain our childhood friendships with those who have gone astray.

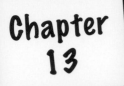

Chapter 13

I GET MARRIED AND HAVE KIDS

DRAWING LESSON:
Draw a life figure.

WHAT YOU WILL NEED:

- Charcoal pencils
- Pastel crayons or Conté crayons. Set of colors
- Spray fixative, matte, not gloss
- Pad of drawing paper suitable for charcoal

THE LESSON

Anatomy is the analytical study of the human body. Medical professionals, scientists, and artists must know and understand anatomy. Life drawing is the interpretation of how a body relates to the world. The body's mathematical composition is (usually) exacting. An adult human is eight heads tall, for example. The foot is the length of the forearm. The wingspan equals the height, with rare exceptions.

I learned, during a class in drawing nudes, that life drawing seeks to find the greater meaning of the form. The poetry of movement. A dancer's body, even in the stillness of a drawing, should convey a readiness to dance.

Drawing from nudes feels majestic. When I did it in that one class, I immediately felt like Chagall and Manet were no longer just strangers in a book, but artists I could now understand and better relate to.

That life-drawing class has served me well as a professional cartoonist. My comic strip features men, women, children, and animals. Understanding the body is key to designing characters that readers accept as real. Even when a female is dressed in sweats and a loose-fitting top, her body is nothing like a man's body. Women usually sit with their knees touching. Many men look for every opportunity to open up at the knees, to rest elbows on knees, to lean forward aggressively. A teenage body slouches predictably in a chair. A small child sits crossed-legged on the floor. An elderly character may bend slightly at the waist when walking. Authenticity is necessary because inaccuracies in art interfere with how well the writing is received. Bad art is a speed bump that disrupts the illusion that Joe, Marcy, and the rest of the cast are a "real family."

I have included this anatomy and life-drawing story because it is part of my journey and artistic process. I have not drawn from a nude model since those classes back in the early '80s. I do not recommend that you, the reader of this book, talk a friend or loved one into posing nude for you. What I do recommend is that you, as an interested student of the arts, pay attention to the human form with new eyes. Look at the way a toddler walks, the way a man leans against a wall, the way a woman enters a car.

If you are an adult and are interested in drawing or painting nudes, I strongly suggest signing up for a structured class. Many art colleges offer such programs. It is risky to attempt any of this at home, even with a spouse. Things can become . . . complicated!

All right. Let's start the lesson. You may draw a pet (if it will sit still), or ask a friend to sit still for a few minutes—fully clothed! Even if the result of this exercise doesn't turn out looking great, you will learn more about "seeing" as opposed to just "looking."

Use a single light source to create highlighted areas and areas that fall into shadow. You will be tempted to overthink certain areas like the fingers and the face (if drawing a person), but try to move through the process without getting bogged down in the details. You want to see the "whole person," capturing the feeling of your model in a state of relaxed contemplation. Charcoal is perfectly suited for life drawing. Your work will look dramatic, even if you are a beginner.

Have your model strike a pose that he or she can easily repeat if there's a need to take a break. Using the tip of your charcoal, swiftly and lightly indicate the head position, and the neck and spinal inclination. Use the horizontal lift of the shoulders to get a sense of the hanging or folding of the arms.

Remember the lesson on geometric shapes in Chapter 1? Use the discipline of seeing the geometry of the torso and pelvis. The turn of the hips, lightly hinted at with the charcoal tip.

(Charcoal can be covered with heavier strokes later but cannot be erased ever, so avoid making distracting marks that cannot be later covered.)

When indicating the hands and feet, remember the size of them. Hands are as large as the face. Feet are as long as the forearm.

When rendering the face, sweep your charcoal right into the dark, shadowy areas of the face, avoiding areas that are illuminated by light. Do the same under the chin and into the drape and folds of your model's clothing.

After sweeping into the darkest areas, lighten your pressure on the charcoal. You will be doing mid-tones now: the eyes, features, and hair. Fingers should be thought of as individual cylinders with roundness created by shadows underneath and with a transition to light on top.

Do not worry much about background items like windows and furniture. A life figure drawing is just what it sounds like.

To enhance the dimensionality of a charcoal drawing. I suggest a final step. Using white conté crayon or chalk, hit the nose tip, the whites of the eyes, or highlights in the hair. The whites should really pop. I used to enjoy working on gray paper to make the white highlights stand out even more.

MY LIFE: SEEING MY CHILDREN BORN WITH HEALTH CHALLENGES

I was married at twenty-four, in 1986, just one year out of college. For me, this proved to be too early. Others may have different opinions, but I think no one should marry before thirty. Give yourself time to develop a bit more maturity before taking on life's hardest and most important job: raising kids.

I married around the same time as some of my friends. It sounds insane to say this, but marriage felt like an "in" thing to do. Looking back now, I wonder how I could have approached something as serious as marriage with the same trend-inspired compulsion as buying an iPad. I treated marriage as the next logical step after graduating from college and landing that first career job.

For awhile, we were, indeed, happy together. We welcomed into our lives two gifts from God. Tess was born on July 16, 1993, which happened to be my mother's birthday. She would have been sixty-one. This coincidence did not sit well with my wife, who had some sort of problem with the long-dead mother-in-law she had never met. Wives almost traditionally chafe at mothers-in-law—two women in one man's life. My mother, of course, had been dead for years, but she was always in my thoughts. She had been an incredibly loving and powerful influence in my early life. Old family baggage can sometimes help torpedo your later relationships.

Tess was born with a form of sickle cell disease, which is genetic and most common to persons of sub-Saharan African descent. It results in abnormally shaped (like a sickle) red blood cells. The cells not only don't carry enough oxygen, but also get tangled in narrow blood vessels, causing problems such as muscle aches, joint problems, and excruciating pain. My brother Mark and sister Cheryle also had the disease, while both my first wife and I were carriers showing no symptoms.

It's a scary disease. It can be life altering and debilitating and used to be fatal to a good portion of those with it. A 1973 University of Maryland study noted that the average victim died at age fourteen. In the years since, treatments have improved and by 2012 that lifespan had extended to fifty years and was still increasing—thanks to better understanding of treatment forms and genetics.

Tess at age twenty-one, with me near her apartment in San Diego in 2014. She grew into a beautiful young lady and is the spitting image of her mom.

But in 1993, when Tess was born, the doctor told me—I can never forget this—"You're both great, young parents. You can have another kid. Don't worry about it." Right. Don't worry about a beautiful daughter's crippling disease because she'll be dead soon and your replacement kid might be healthier. Good bedside manner there, Doc.

Tess was fortunate, having almost no symptoms growing up. She would be asymptomatic for years, but big temperature differences could trigger massive problems.

She had two episodes, when she was five and six years old, and both were terrifying. In the first—and this is typical of the disease—she had some common cold. The sniffles. But suddenly she became dehydrated and lethargic, and we rushed her to the hospital just in time to save her. Kids can go down fast, especially while small. I wasn't present at the second episode; she was at summer camp, and they had to airlift her to the hospital.

Being a father is the most terrifying, frightening thing sometimes. No matter how well things are going, when the kids are out there, no longer under your protection, it's scary, and never really out of your thoughts.

But Tess is in her twenties now, has a good job in San Diego, and has not had another major problem.

Rex was born on September 29, 1997, and he was most definitely not a "replacement" for Tess. But he was born with two clubfeet—bilateral clubfeet. I knew there was something odd the moment he emerged into the world. The soles of his feet faced each other, turned inward.

This is potentially extremely bad. The body is a delicate and beautifully choreographed mechanism. Think of the line from the song "Dem Bones": "the knee bone's connected to the thigh bone." Everything's connected, and so people with clubfeet may also have a variety of other problems, some very serious. Rex had a small problem with his palate and teeth, but seems to have been spared the other side effects.

We sucked it up and got the best health coverage we could and paid a lot of it out of pocket—tens of thousands of dollars for surgeries. Poor Rex had to

Rex sitting with me at the drawing board in October 1997. He was just one month old and had just endured the first of many surgeries to correct his clubfeet.

endure many, many operations as he grew, and he spent the majority of his youth in some state of repair—with casts, often in a wheelchair—as they straightened his feet, realigned his hips, and got his spine as straight as possible.

But his road was not easy. One incident stands out in my mind. Rex was stoic about his problems and almost never complained about the pain. When he was thirteen, he went on an eighth-grade class field trip to Disneyland. I was worried—I always worried about Rex and Tess—but he wanted to go so badly that we let him. When my wife Crystal and I went to meet Rex's bus at the end of the day, all the other kids got off the bus and ran to their parents' cars. Crystal and I were staring at the bus through the windshield. No Rex. Then, just as I was about to get out of the car, he hobbled off the bus. Crystal lost it then. She broke out crying. Bawling. She wept in the car, trying to compose herself while Rex slowly, slowly limped his way to us, grimacing in pain at every step. And he still had three and a half more years of procedures to go through.

One time after one of the many surgeries, I said to Rex, "You are my hero." I don't know of any father who ever said that to his son, but I thought, we're put on this earth to give our kids strong, healthy egos. Maybe his standing up awkwardly on his own two feet for the first time was, for him, what my Fred Flintstone moment was for me. Ugly, poorly done, but a start and, with a parent's support and love, and a lot of internal grit and determination, something that could be improved upon until he stood and walked normally.

Today Rex not only has normal teeth and a walk that is ninety-five percent normal, but he runs around and loves skateboarding. He's amazing. By the time he graduated from high school, in 2015, he had become a strapping young man.

Correcting Rex's spine and legs took time, though. A side effect of spending your youth as a wheelchair-bound kid with legs in casts is that the other kids in school will bully you. Being confined to a wheelchair and unable to walk, Rex spent a lot of years as an overweight, chubby boy.

Rex was at one point so helpless that even the girls would ambush him and tip over his wheelchair and laugh as he cried out in pain. I talked to school officials and teachers about this. They just shrugged and gave me a "What can you do? Kids are just that way" response.

This could have altered my perception of America's youth. But by then I was often speaking to large groups of kids at schools, summer camps, and so on, and I had a broader perspective. I spoke to the kids at Rex's school, giving a speech about bullying. Nothing helped. It was just a terrible thing to witness. Rex is an unusually sweet guy, an admirable human being. He's so kind. I've never met a child so loving despite the fact that in school people were never nice to

Rex, in high school. Sometimes, looking at him feels like looking into a mirror.

him. I eventually taught Rex some moves I had learned in my own karate classes and during my street-fighting days as a kid. (I lost a lot of those fights, but one of the beauties of being a dad is that the facts don't always matter!) One day, Rex turned on an attacker and bloodied the boy's nose. I was called in to the school. They told me they would suspend Rex. After my previous visits—begging them to stop the bullying—and then their ignoring it, they were now going to suspend the victim for daring to fight back. I told them they'd have to suspend *me* because I had ordered Rex to do just what he did. Ultimately, they decided to do nothing at all. Rex was not bullied after that. Most bullies are cowards inside and usually don't attack anyone who resists.

Life Lesson: Pay attention.

When you become a parent, you must accept a new reality in which your children's needs take first priority. All children—whether healthy or sick—need attentive, responsive parents. And, as in our life drawing, the human eye has vision, too, but the mind has to be trained to detect detail. The brain has to be trained to deal with the vision, promptly and adequately. Fail to react to what you're seeing around you, and disaster may follow. If a single procedure or surgery for Rex had been put off or delayed, it could have had life-altering consequences for him.

So see what needs to be dealt with and handle it at once. This is what parenthood is really all about.

Chapter 14

I LEARN TO TELL THE STORY

DRAWING LESSON:
Draw a crowd.

WHAT YOU WILL NEED:

- Markers (existing supplies, Flairs, and Sharpies for large areas)
- Pad of drawing paper

THE LESSON

Go to a place where crowds gather, perhaps outside a church. When you see the crowd, you may be afraid to begin drawing. Crowds are intimidating. Drawing one can seem like a lot of work.

Notice that the crowd itself has a shape. Quickly draw that shape, just a rough outline. Now all the people have to fit inside that shape, so they can be smaller than if you were drawing them individually. A crowd is easier to draw than a single person, because an individual person contains much more detail. Try to find the extremes within the crowd: the tallest guy, the tiniest boy, for example. Focus on them, because they stand out. The other people are not individually important; you just need a crowd of people, figures, to fill it out. Add the dark places, the shadowy areas within the crowd. See how quickly the crowd takes shape? It's not so scary after all.

MY LIFE: THE BOY WHO USED TO STUTTER NOW SOUNDS OFF TO THE CROWD.

My career as a public speaker started when I met John Trombetta in 1993. He called me and invited me to come and speak to a crowd of young people at something called PFEW. Speak? To a crowd? Of kids? And what's a PFEW?

John explained. Pennsylvania Free Enterprise Week is a summer camp for high-school juniors that teaches them about free enterprise as a foundation for America. It's put on each summer by the Foundation for Free Enterprise Education. The foundation is based in Erie, Pennsylvania, but the camps are held at Lycoming College and the Pennsylvania College of Technology, both in Williamsport, Pennsylvania. I do talks at each campus as needed. Each summer camp runs for five separate week-long sessions, and each student attends for one week. I asked John what the gig paid. He said I could eat all the grilled cheese sandwiches I could stomach. You don't get offers like that every day, so I said that of course I'd do it.

John had never heard me speak and had never even met me until moments before my first speech at PFEW. He actually had no idea that I was worth even a cheese sandwich. But a friend of his had heard me speak at another event, heard my life story as I told it, and called John and recommended me.

For that first meeting, I drove from Philadelphia up to Williamsport. The three-hour drive took me through the Pocono Mountains. So remote was the highway that I saw a full-grown black bear standing by the side of the road. The bear seemed to wave at me as if to wish me good luck.

I felt out of my league at the event. The other speakers were captains of industry, corporate giants with titles so long their business cards were printed on both sides. When I first met John, he asked me what I planned to talk about. I told him I didn't have a clue, that it was all in God's hands. I was serious; I hadn't rehearsed anything.

"I'm a cartoonist," I squeaked to the audience.

My nervousness was impossible to mask onstage. I muddled through forty-five minutes, and the applause was kind. I had three hours to drive home and think about everything I had done wrong. I was certain I'd never be invited back to PFEW. I was also relieved not to see the bear on my return trip. I didn't want him to ask me how it went.

About a week later, I received a letter from a sixteen-year-old girl named Sheila. She said she had enjoyed my speech tremendously, but had been too nervous to approach me to let me know. (Too bad; I could have used her encouragement.) Sheila said she could relate to my life story. She said her story was tragic and discouraging. She then made a startling confession: "Mr. Armstrong, you spoke on a Thursday. My suicide was fully planned out for Saturday, two days later." She wrote that I'd given her hope. She went into disturbing detail about her sexually abusive father and her brother's suicide a year earlier. She'd recently discovered that her ten-year-old sister had also been sexually abused by their sick father, and she had decided to end it all.

But then she heard my story and felt a newfound hope.

Sheila thanked me for convincing her to go to college and pursue her dreams. We stayed in touch briefly, through her senior year. I don't know if she achieved her dream of college, but I hope she did.

Since then, several more kids have told me that I talked them out of suicide. I've learned to follow up on those. Carefully. I get in touch with the parents first and then, if they agree, to the kid. The most important part is to get the kid some help; *who* provides the help is not important.

I suppose that John liked me after all. I've been doing PFEW talks, all five sessions each year, for more than twenty years now. I tell the kids about my life, the ghetto, the importance of education, the value of single-minded determination to succeed, and the need to stay on what I call "the upper road," and not to fall down to the "lower road" that is filled with the potholes of drugs, laziness, and other bad behaviors.

I began my second career as a public speaker in 1993, thanks to John Trombetta, posing here with me in 2013 (inset).

I was given this bobblehead doll to commemorate my twentieth year of PFEW.

The staff puts up a big paper background for me, across the entire rear of the stage, and during an hour of talking, jumping around, I fill that canvas with cartoon characters and other drawings. The audience, each and every time, goes from laughing hysterically to crying and then back again. It's a very emotional talk, for them and for me. I've seen John standing off to one side, weeping, and he's heard me talk some ninety times.

I now live in Los Angeles and fly back East to do those talks. No more driving up from Philadelphia through the mountains. But, if I were to see that bear again, I'd tell him it worked out all right, that I found that my life story could have value to a few young kids who were facing horrible situations at home.

Life Lesson: Embrace your struggles.

Sometimes I meet kids who wish they were someone else. Someone living an easier life. Sometimes they wish to be a famous singer or actor.

The fact is, you alone are uniquely qualified to handle your own life, problems and all. And you can now learn and grow from your adversity. You have not been cursed with struggles. Rather, a life without struggle is an invisible curse.

When I realized that my struggles, and my telling of them, could help someone, I felt my true purpose unfolding. Though we are all different, we all share this one thing: everyone suffers.

Talking to others about my life and how I have dealt with my problems has shown me that I can really make a difference in a short amount of time. Perhaps you, too, can help others by telling them about your life and how you overcame problems. It requires the courage to speak your personal truth, but it's yet another way—and a very powerful way—of giving back. And giving back is what life is all about. As Dot Armstrong taught me, give it all away. Every bit. Save nothing for tomorrow because you may not have a tomorrow.

Most people are terrified of public speaking. They don't want to end up looking silly in front of a crowd. It's the perceived power of collective scrutiny. We don't think about saying something embarrassing in front of one or two people, but when it's time to address a congregation, we are frozen with trepidation and self-criticism.

It may sound odd, but a room tends to be kinder than one or two people. A room is not going to taunt or ridicule you. A room won't push you over in a wheelchair, or mock you. A room won't contradict you. Quite the opposite. A room cheers for you. It feels empathy for you and wants you to win.

This experience, early in my career, defined success for me. It informed me that success can mask itself as failure for a time. Though I came away from that first speech feeling like I had failed, I had had a positive impact on someone else in the world. Not everything you say will be so portentous as to deter a young person from suicide. But, you never really know, do you?

Chapter 15

MY MARRIAGE—AND MY LIFE—COLLAPSE

DRAWING LESSON:
Create a colorful still life of a bowl of fruit.

WHAT YOU WILL NEED:

- Charcoal pencils
- Pastel crayons or Conté crayons. Set of colors
- Pad of drawing paper
- Lamp
- Bowl of mixed fruit
- Large scarf or cloth
- Spray fixative, matte

THE LESSON

On a table, drape the scarf with soft folds, and set the bowl of fruit on it. Use a bowl with no pattern because this exercise is all about the fruit. Now shine the lamp on this setup. (From the side is best, so that there are highlights and contrasting shadows.)

Now, with your charcoal pencil, draw the outline of the objects. The lamp has given you a nice single-light source (you may even decide to turn out other lights to accentuate the single-lighting). As you sketch the outline, use the edge of your charcoal pencil to add shadowing in spots the light doesn't reach. Now add color, lightly at first; you can always add more but you can't take away too much. Avoid adding color where the light hits the fruit the strongest. Go slowly with pastels. They are not as forgiving as paint.

We are using pastels because they are texturally similar to fruit. Pastels look like chalk but are not as brittle. Blending pastels is easier than blending chalk. Blending is a must and can be done with your fingers.

Like charcoal, pastels cannot be erased. When applying pastels, work with the lightest colors first, and then work into the shadows with the darker tones. It's the opposite of working with acrylics or oils. On light paper, this means the highlighted areas are not even touched until the work is almost complete. A pastel set comes with a white pastel, which can be used to accent your piece when the art is nearly complete.

Pastels are messy, and pastel paper is not cheap, so move slowly. A pastel drawing of a bowl of fruit can take days or even weeks to complete. There is no rush to finish this, or any piece of art (unless you are a syndicated cartoonist).

A bowl of fruit is soft, vulnerable in the way human beings are. As you work, strive to achieve the illusion that you could pick up each piece of fruit, bite into it, and juice would squirt out. Turn the still life into something relatable and human. A banana is smooth on the outside, but inside, it's also vulnerable.

No two fruits are alike. Apples, oranges, peaches, all have an individual character. Grapes are fraternal and come in groups. I instructed you to use a bowl of mixed fruit—an apple, a peach, a plum, grapes, banana, an orange, for example—because the variety creates an excellent exercise. The plum should not end up looking like an apple, and grapes should not resemble tiny plums strung together. Pay attention to each type of fruit as you draw.

When all your colors are on the paper and you are satisfied with the bowl of fruit—when each piece of fruit looks good enough to eat—spray the entire drawing with a matte fixative, which will keep your final artwork from smudging accidentally. There is also a gloss fixative, but that will make your fruit look too shiny. You don't want a shiny bowl of fruit, unless, perhaps, the entire bowl is filled with apples and oranges.

If you decide to frame your pastel drawing, don't cover it in shiny glass. Use a frame without glass, or buy a special no-shine glass.

Now it's time to admire your effort. The bowl of fruit is a living model. The fruit has texture, juice, vivid colors.

By the way, the one-source light means you see things from a single, narrow perspective. This can be a good thing in a painting or a photograph. It's not such a good thing in a marriage.

My Life: Marriage and Divorce

By 2001, I thought I had it all: I was working as both a syndicated cartoonist and a sometime freelance art director. This meant lots of responsibility, but also a high income. We bought expensive toys and had accumulated friends, cars, a big house with a big mortgage, and a reputation as a classy power couple. Not only was I living my dream as a cartoonist, but I was also a sought-after motivational speaker, appearing in magazine and television interviews for the likes of *Time*, *People*, and *Good Morning America*, just to name a few. I had more money than I ever dreamed possible for a boy from the gang-ridden streets of West Philly.

Then I realized that my marriage wasn't as terrific as I believed. Having grown up without an adult marital relationship to model, I was in over my head, despite my education and intellectual readiness to settle down. Simply put, my wife was not happy, and somehow I had missed it. She'd attempted to let me know a thousand ways—explicit, implicit, obvious, and subtle. Yet somehow I still didn't see it.

I was blind, willfully blind, and saw only what I wanted to see from my limited perspective. And by the time I woke up to the problems in my marriage, it was too little, too late.

Here are the pitfalls that torpedoed my first marriage:

Fatigue. Marriage tired me out. It is relentlessly demanding, and you get zero time off. When you're single and dating, the dating process is fed by your wants, your desires. But once married, your individual needs and wants are not what feed the marriage. Marriage is about attention to your spouse; it's about compromise. Being single is all self-interest; marriage is all sacrifice.

Throughout the 1990s, I built a reputation as a public speaker. This is a reception, held in 1996, at the Glendale, California, corporate headquarters of Nestlé USA, Inc., which recognized me as one of their "Men of Courage." I'm signing a commemorative book for a young fan.

Neglect. We crave recognition and attention from each other, and from the outside world. As I became more and more recognized for being the creator of a hot new comic strip, my wife began to feel less and less recognized and under-appreciated. My wife had a career, too, and quite a successful one. But her work didn't get her the same level of public attention.

It is understandable, and I don't blame her. If I had spent the early years of our marriage watching my wife glorified for her work while I toiled in anonymity, I would not have been a happy camper. But, as it happened, I was more than happy. I was giddy, and oblivious to my young wife suffering from neglect.

Don't get me wrong, I made all of the gestures that are required of a hus-band. Bushels of flowers. Limos to the theater on Valentine's Day. Trips to Paris, Mexico, and Africa. Love, however, is not demonstrated by material goods. It is demonstrated by gestures, large and small, by daily self-sacrifice. Love is easy to say, but the truth is you have to put your spouse first. Sometimes that means you have to show the other person that you actually prefer that he or she is happy, instead of you.

By the year 2000, I had grown oblivious to warning signs that all was not well at home. Somehow, I was failing to notice that my own wife hated reading *JumpStart*.

Then, to top it all off, Tiger Woods came between us.

Selfishness. No, of course Tiger Woods didn't destroy my marriage. But he fostered in me a fascination with golf.

I had never played golf, but, like almost everyone else, I was astounded by this man who came to dominate the privileged world of golf. I set out to be Tiger Woods, if only in my own mind. I wasn't all that good at it; my play was average, around a handicap of 17. But on the driving range, I was a beast. I often hit the ball over the farthest fence. (Too bad that golf is more than just the driving range.) Golf became my mistress, my addiction. When you're married, some immaturity can creep in at times. You look out for adultery and other things that you're told (and rightly so) can destroy your marriage. But selfishness sometimes creeps in under your radar. And golf (or any obsession) is an inherently selfish activity.

The writer Anaïs Nin once wrote, of marriage:

> *Love never dies a natural death. It dies because we don't know how to replenish its source. It dies of blindness and errors and betrayals. It dies of illness and wounds; it dies of weariness, of witherings, of tarnishings.*

I believe in marriage. I believe in marriage so much, I've done it twice. My first wife and I were married for sixteen years, the majority of them—so I had thought—happy, prosperous, and enviable. We had two beautiful, well-adjusted children, legions of friends, associates, and admirers. No extramarital affairs. And all of that was lost when our marriage came to a disastrous end in 2003. I suggested that we divorce and she acted upon that instantly. I was served with papers within days.

It was an absolute train wreck, occurring in slow motion. The injuries to all involved were excruciating, deliberate, and preventable.

I believe that divorce is supremely wicked. But it happened anyway. Life's most valuable lessons are sometimes taught in arenas that are extreme, with harsh cruelty, played out in public view like a Roman Coliseum gore-fest. At one point I even asked Jesus to stop the pain. Know what he said? "Is that you, Robb? Long time. Thought you'd lost my number . . . "

Here's what I learned about marriage as a result of all that wreckage:

- Wait to get married until you have some life experience, know yourself, and are happy with yourself, and look for those traits in the person who will be your life partner.

- Marry someone who accepts you as you are, imperfections and all. People don't change.

- Get married when you have reached that stage in life where you're ready to fully commit to lifelong service to another human being.

- And marriage is for better or worse, so don't marry someone unless you have seen him or her at the worst—and know that the worst is something you can stand.

I also learned that divorce can act as a sort of filter. It filters out your true friends from the people who just smile and pretend. It reveals much about the personalities of everyone involved, including the bystanders. During most divorces, a couple's mutual friends are forced to choose which of you to side with and which of you to delete from their memories. You divide up your property, and you divide up your friends.

In our case, there wasn't that much dividing of either. She got the big house, the children, and the contents. For some odd reason the judge even gave her a lot of my original comic-strip drawings. Why she even wanted them, I cannot guess.

And she got all of our mutual friends and even a few from my childhood. I moved on, away from her, away from fair-weather friends, away from what I had long thought would be my happy and forever family life. I moved into an apartment in another part of town and was grateful for the few friends who stuck by me.

I also had problems with creditors. I was not originally very good with money. I tended to spend without a thought to my bank balance. Maybe it was a psychological reaction to having grown up so poor. One of the many unfair burdens I had put on my wife was managing the family finances.

After the divorce, I discovered that I seemed to owe just about everyone. I also had problems with the IRS, who were actually very kind to me and not at all the ogres I'd been told they could be. It took time, time and scrimping on my part but, eventually, I learned how to take responsibility for my finances. I now have a financial manager.

I learned something else during this stressful time. I learned that I liked being alone, that I wasn't bothered by loneliness. Self-sufficiency is important to a person who works alone and not in some crowded office. It turned out that I loved solitude, loved being alone with my thoughts. I sat in my little apartment with nothing in it, and I was so happy. It was a chance to reinvent everything about myself, a chance to look in the mirror, both literally and figuratively.

And I especially cherished my weekend opportunities with my kids, learning to be present with them instead of just in the house with them. I learned that fatherhood could be a lot of fun. I'd make up funny, outrageous stories while driving my kids on road trips to Atlantic City and other places.

I also learned that a cheap apartment was just as good a shelter for me as a big McMansion. I learned that thrift stores sold good clothes if I knew how to look. I learned how to handle a checkbook. I learned that I needed to look for a responsible, mature, self-fulfilled woman to be my life's partner.

In short, I learned how to become an adult, a good father, a man.

Life Lesson: Face the truth and recognize what's happening around you.

When my work—establishing *JumpStart* and getting it syndicated—became my priority, I developed tunnel vision. I saw what was in front of me, but failed to notice the other hues that were really part of the same picture.

This is desirable in our drawing lesson with a bowl of fruit; we focus on that and not on the table it's sitting on or the room it's in. But in real life—and nothing is more real in life than marriage—too much focus here means not enough focus there. Marriage is all-in, all the time, everywhere, all at once. But if you can see the whole picture and not just part of the picture, and participate fully in the experience, you will see, do, and enjoy wonderful things, indeed.

AN ANGEL COMES INTO MY LIFE

DRAWING LESSON:
Make a bad painting better.

WHAT YOU WILL NEED:

- A bad painting (framed)
- Masking or painter's tape
- Pad of drawing paper
- Gesso
- Brushes. Various sizes of sabeline (ox hair) or camel hair high-quality brushes
- Beginner's set of water-based acrylic paints
- Dry rags
- Two small cans full of water

THE LESSON

Go to Goodwill or to a thrift store and buy a horrid piece of framed art for five bucks (or less!). Make sure it's worthless and not an early lost masterpiece by Caravaggio. In fact, the worse the painting the better, and if you can lay your hands on one of those mass-produced prints, perfect!

First, cover the frame in tape. The painting is not the frame's fault. Next, coat the old painting in gesso. Once a canvas is covered in gesso—a thick, viscous film usually colored white—you can use anything on it, charcoal, acrylics, oils, whatever. The gesso dries quickly, so add enough layers of gesso to cover the underlying painting or canvas surface.

At this point, you have had enough art lessons—fifteen of them—to paint anything you want on the new surface. It can be a bowl of fruit, a nude, or a landscape. It can even be a self-portrait. For this lesson, we're using acrylics, but the subject is entirely up to you. Just be sure it is an improvement over what used to be there.

"Why am I painting over a painting?" you ask? Well, it's not to just replicate the original in a sort of paint-by-the-numbers way. That bad painting deserves to be obliterated. Painting over it will make the world a better place, and each of us is put on this earth to make the world a better place. Bad art does not serve the planet at all.

And, yes, I hear you saying, "But my art is probably just as bad. Maybe worse." No, it isn't. It's good because it's genuine, because it's from you. Because it's who you are. I guarantee it will be better.

By the way, I'm not the inventor of this idea. Artists often re-use materials, sometimes because the materials are expensive and the artist poor. An artist may have a commission to do a mural and—guess what?—there's already a mural on that wall. So he shrugs, paints gesso over the first mural, and paints another on top in order to earn his commission. Or perhaps the artist is dissatisfied with the first try and wants to do better the second time. Michelangelo, for example, destroyed his first version of the Sistine Chapel ceiling and did it over.

So paint away over an old artwork. Happily.

MY LIFE: ROBB ARMSTRONG, REDUX

After my divorce, I immediately went to work reinventing myself. I moved to Conshohocken, a pretty suburb north of Philadelphia. I rented an apartment. I took control of my finances. And I hit the gym.

The gym helped me get in shape both physically and mentally. I would lift the weights, working past the sweat, the muscle strain, the pain by saying to myself—sometimes out loud—"They can't take this away from me. They can take my house, my car, everything I have invested in. But they can't have this."

I grew out my afro. The transformation became noticeable after only a couple of months. I went to the mall and ran into a married couple I had known for a long time. Though the husband and I were childhood friends, I'd lost them to my wife in the divorce—along with the antique furniture.

When I brushed past this couple at the mall, they did not recognize me. I was in shape. I was dressed in a thrift-store T-shirt and fashionably worn-out jeans. I looked ten years younger than when they had last seen me. I was content. We exchanged pleasantries and went our separate ways. For life.

This pattern continues to repeat itself to this day. I am often unrecognizable to people I have known for years. I appear to be aging backward—sort of like F. Scott Fitzgerald's Benjamin Button. My face is reluctant to wrinkle. My hair is still stubbornly dark. I am happy for everything I have and am a better steward when it comes to money. I no longer use lines of credit to feed my status or my ego. And I still adore shopping at thrift stores.

And I believe in loving someone at her worst.

While visiting my former college roommate, Rico Hernandez, he introduced me to his friend, Crystal Spruell, a beautiful young lady with striking green eyes and a peaceful disposition. Crystal was born in Washington, DC, but was raised by her grandparents in North Carolina.

She is a great conversationalist, easy-going, and fun. I needed that when I met her, someone to have fun with. Crystal is family-oriented. I observed how effortlessly her love for family seemed to flow through her very soul. I aspire toward that. She doesn't judge. She doesn't presume. She doesn't posture. She doesn't crave one-upmanship.

My wedding day to Crystal, August 25, 2007.

She also became loyal and defensive of me soon after our courtship began. I knew, despite having once thought that I'd never marry again, that Crystal would be my wife. Not "wife number two" but my wife, in every sense of the word. She's not perfect. Just perfect for me. God had sent an angel to save me.

We had a long-distance romance for a few years and married in 2007. I scraped together what money I had—debts be damned—and bought a house in Conshohocken. It was a single-family, split-level house, with a little bit of land and a lawn to mow and snow to shovel. I did a lot of interior work—painting and some unique wall coverings. One thing I had learned in the advertising business was good taste in colors and textures. It felt good to create a home with Crystal, because, at last, I felt I had nothing to prove to anyone.

I especially enjoyed spending time in the South, visiting Crystal's family. Life in North Carolina is totally different from life in Philly. The front-porch country lifestyle there is as close to Utopia as modern man is ever going to get. Everything fades away in their kitchen, as Nancy, Crystal's grandmother, cooks up the family's favorite "chicken pastry," and the screen door acts more like a revolving door for endless visitors and family members. Being just "one of the family" in this world is without question one of the highlights of my life. I copied that feeling by adding a large cast of characters to *JumpStart*.

Crystal is shown here with Nancy (standing), her grandmother, who helped raise her, and Lucy, her great-grandmother, who lived to be 100.

Before I met Crystal I was separated, awaiting finalization of the divorce, living in an apartment. I would hang out with my buddies and drink beer and watch ball on television. Sometimes I was happy about this; sometimes I was miserable. Once she and I were together every day, I was a new person. We didn't have a lot of money, but we always enjoyed each other's company.

I remember taking Crystal to her first ballgame. The Baltimore Orioles. Our seats at Camden Yards were bad, and I was embarrassed. "I'm sorry for these seats," I told her. "It's all I can afford right now."

Crystal said, "Why are you apologizing? I'm right next to you. I've got the best seat in the house!"

I know it's only coincidence, but she reminds me of the Langston Hughes poem I mentioned earlier: *Well, son, I'll tell you: Life for me ain't been no crystal stair.*

Maybe Crystal is my stairway to becoming a better man. Maybe she's my stair to heaven.

I also have worked very hard to be a good husband. I had a lot to prove to myself. I didn't like the way my first marriage had turned out. I disliked having what I considered to be a massive, glaring failure in my life. Now I consciously think of ways to put my family first.

A husband (and wife too, I suppose) should know his or her shortcomings and limitations. I'm poor at logistical details. I used to accidentally double-book engagements and other duties. I hired someone to help me with my professional speaking dates, and now my booking agent Donna Leavy makes my life better by focusing me on the overall task rather than on the details surrounding that task. Thankfully, Crystal is an extremely patient person and handles the social events.

Now, I realize that I'm an atypical Black man. I'm not your average cat. The fact is, I've led such a broad and sweeping life, so rich at one point, so poor at others. (Entertainer Sophie Tucker once said, "I've been rich and I've been poor. Rich is better," and I know how she felt.) I've lived in worlds so white, so Black. I've been so professional, so country, so ordinary, so extraordinary. In one week I can go from famous to anonymous, from crowds of hundreds listening to every word I say to three friends in a room disapproving of something I did. It's humbling. And it's filled me with gratitude.

Life Lesson: Try every day to be better.

Your best idea is your next idea. Isn't that marvelous? A friend once called me to complain about a television show that appeared to have stolen material from *JumpStart*. I said, "That's what *JumpStart* is here for." Take it, world. I'm a contributor. And, besides, that's not my best work. You haven't see my best stuff yet—and neither have I.

Never give up on your most important project, the project of *you*. You can improve. If you stumble today, well, there's always tomorrow. As Frank Sinatra once sang, pick yourself up, get back in the race. You don't have to win the race, but get up and run hard without worrying about who is in front of or behind you.

Perhaps the weirdest thing about divorce is that two intelligent people who believe in God and in his miraculous power to heal and intervene, have said to one another, "You can't improve. Your best days are behind you. I am going to find someone better."

Obviously divorce is absurd on that level. The new person will also be a work in progress. The difference is that we're shocked at what happened the first time and we try harder the second time.

So keep getting better. Don't be discouraged. Take heart knowing that the good stuff is yet to come. The best stuff is still in you. No one can take it because you have not yet thought of it. Your best idea is your next idea.

Chapter 17

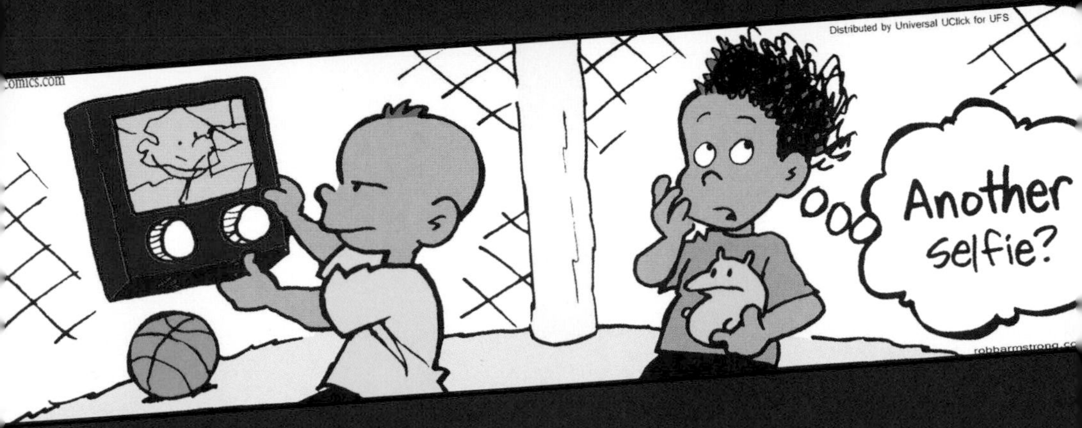
Distributed by Universal UClick for UFS
Another selfie?

I AM LA BOUND

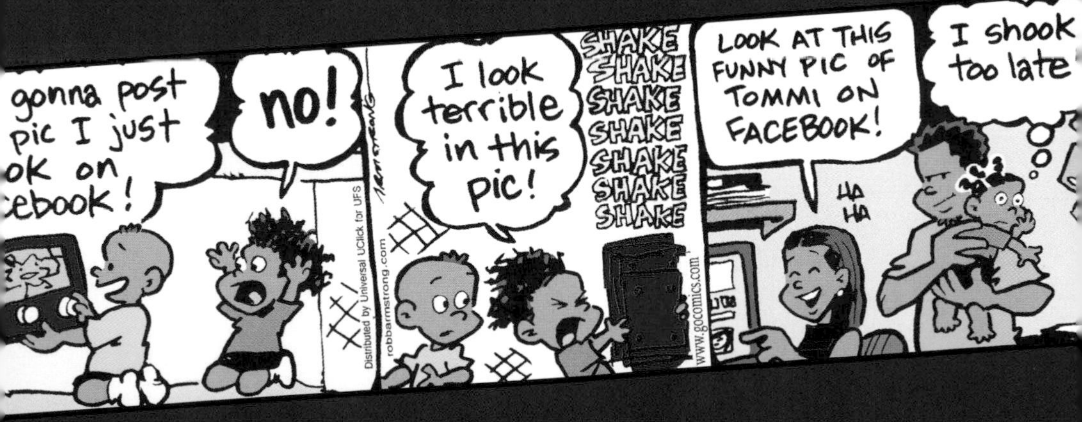
gonna post
pic I just
ok on
ebook!
no!
I look terrible in this pic!
SHAKE
SHAKE
SHAKE
SHAKE
SHAKE
SHAKE
SHAKE
LOOK AT THIS FUNNY PIC OF TOMMI ON FACEBOOK!
HA HA
I shook too late
Distributed by Universal UClick for UFS
robbarmstrong.com
www.gocomics.com

DRAWING LESSON:
Make a collage.

WHAT YOU WILL NEED:

- Foam board. Buy several in 24x36-inch size or larger (one to use, one or two spares). Color doesn't matter. Don't buy the cork version, it's more fragile and it generates tiny cork dust.

- A shadow box without glass large enough for one of your foam boards

- Some photographs

- Scissors

- Spray adhesive or Elmer's glue

- Your Sharpie and Flair pens

- Removable tape

- Large workspace

THE LESSON

Life is the ultimate collage, and it's a stunning masterpiece. The people you have met, the places you have been, the moments that comprise your time on Earth, when considered together, are nothing short of miraculous. Everyone's life is exciting, and this collage will prove it.

This is a fun art lesson, but it requires a bit of research. If you don't want to destroy original photographs, make color copies of them, or scan them into your computer and then print out copies. Take photos of any three-dimensional objects you'd like to incorporate into your collage.

Packrats rejoice! If you are in the habit of saving everything that has entered into your life, today is your lucky day. If you have been diligently purging your living space of useless knickknacks and other nostalgic mementos, this art lesson may be something of a challenge.

Start with photos. Dust off that old shoebox and drag out the albums. Go through your smartphone and Facebook albums. You are now looking through the life story, in pictures, of the most fascinating human being ever born. Until now, you may have thought that William Shakespeare or Jackie Onassis or Denzel Washington was more fascinating, but that's incorrect.

None of those people was born into your circumstances. None of them loved in the manner that you loved. Being you, for any length of time, is simply too tall an order for anyone but you.

As you sort through boxes, crates, file cabinets, and the attic, keep in mind that you will not be able to include everything that you find.

But because a collage is, by design, somewhat chaotic and unrestrictive in its composition, it may surprise you just how much you can include, especially if you take photographs of individual items.

I created this collage in 2007. It's a repurposed door covered in paint, glue, images, all kinds of stuff.

After you have collected your items, spread them out on a garage or basement floor.

Using removable tape, begin in the center of your foam core and tape down photographs from your early years. Move in a clockwise direction, taping clippings and other articles, trying to be as chronological as possible. Within minutes you will see how interesting your life has been. The collage will begin "piecing itself" together. The collage need not remain flat. You can layer photos and objects as you wish. Find typography or other graphics—art-supply stores sell press-on letters, but you can print out large-size type from your computer for this, too—to help tell the story. A collage can be a living art form, meaning it need not ever reach completion. You can add to it as long as you wish, even for the rest of your life. Your children can add to it, or expand upon it, even after you have passed on.

You may also choose to sign and frame it once you feel it is finished. I suggest a shadow box without glass, so it can be touched and added to. Maintain balance so the collage always appears well thought out.

This collage is spectacular! And consider that it is only a glimpse into the life of the person who made it. It is also unique. Nothing exactly like it will ever exist.

MY LIFE: EXPANDING MY HORIZONS, AND LEARNING NEW SKILLS

After our divorce, I opposed my ex-wife moving to Seattle for a job offer. I had visitation rights and wanted to stay close to Tess and Rex. But when she got a job offer in a town just two hours' drive north of Los Angeles, I agreed to let her take the kids and go.

Then I followed them. I had long thought that my future lay in Hollywood, somehow. Perhaps *JumpStart* could become a television series or a movie. I had already been trying to get some of ideas picked up for television, but I had been completely unsuccessful. Perhaps if I relocated to the center of the action, I'd have a more realistic shot. There was only one way to find out.

So, in 2009 Crystal and I rented out our house in Conshohocken, and we moved to Los Angeles. I had one big advantage over most of the hopeful actors or writers or directors who shared cheap apartments while trying desperately to get work: I already had work. I was making good money—*JumpStart* was syndicated in hundreds of newspapers—and drawing cartoons is a portable job.

And people in Los Angeles, in the Hollywood film business, were willing to help me out. Al Capp's old comic strip *Li'l Abner* used to have a character named Joe Btfsplk who walked around all day, every day, under a dark cloud of bad luck. Lightning sought Joe out. Auto accidents happened around him as he crossed the street. Pianos fell out of windows on him. He was so jinxed that he affected people he walked near. I sometimes feel like the reverse of Joe Btfsplk. I may have a cloud over my head, too, but sitting on that cloud is an angel, who sees to it that I'm blessed. Whenever I need help, people just pop up and pitch in.

My mother was like that too. Maybe it's genetic. Or maybe people just look at me and say to themselves, "That man needs help." Whatever it is, I'm grateful for it. And I try to give back as much as I receive.

Crystal and I rented a townhouse on a cul-de-sac in Pasadena. The dozen houses were inside a gate, and at first the place was almost empty. There was only one other family. Crispin Luna was an outgoing man with a big smile and a hand out to shake. He looked like Tom Cruise, and he made money by starting businesses. He was a champion business-starter, and once he got one going, he sold it and started another.

Crispin Luna and I, shortly after I moved to LA in 2009.

Crispin and his wife, Nora, took a great interest in me and in my family—Crystal as well as Tess and Rex, who came to stay with us every other weekend. He also acted as our guide to Los Angeles and the West Coast.

Crispin was fascinated by my work, though he hadn't read the comic strip. I mean, the man couldn't read a four-panel strip without his mind wandering by panel two. His mind raced. Comic strips are not for everybody, but he was very smart and fun to be around.

Crispin and Nora had three little girls, and two had been born with albinism. Aside from the obvious lack of skin color, this can be a serious problem. One girl had to have serious facial reconstruction, and while both could see somewhat, they were legally blind. I was dealing with a sixteen-year-old daughter with sickle cell disease and a twelve-year-old son getting his feet under him through painful surgeries. The Lunas and the Armstrongs had a lot in common.

When Rex and Tess were not visiting, I could spread out my materials and draw without interruption. One day I was drawing at the kitchen table, when the Luna girls came in. We never locked our doors in our quiet little cul-de-sac. The girls soon had me drawing a pig for them. Then a cat. I pushed aside my comic strip for the moment. I was delighted. But Crispin came in to shoo them off, apologizing to me for my being disturbed. "I'm sorry the kids ran in here like this," he said.

His oldest, Isabel, grabbed some of my markers, apparently planning to take those home with her.

"Isabel, we have plenty of markers at home," Crispin said.

"Yeah," Isabel said. "But ours don't have any drawings in them." In Isabel's six-year-old mind, the markers were magical, with powers allowing me to draw. I sometimes agree!

Crystal and I met a lot of other friends through the Lunas. The Lunas are generous folks. I once complimented Crispin on his watch, and he took it off and gave it to me.

I am blessed to have people like this all around me. Maybe God wants me to be as generous as them. I'm getting there—part of God's love for me is his tutelage—and I do aspire toward that, to be both generous to my loved ones and to leave this life with a philanthropic legacy.

Our town house was not big, and in addition to Crystal and me, we squeezed in two kids every other weekend. My office space was tiny and cramped, and working at home had distractions. So, of course, Crispin Luna stepped up once more.

He offered me space in his office. It was fabulous, located in the upstairs of an old brick building that was a converted train station in the Old Pasadena Historic District. The office faced an alley. To me, Philadelphia-ghetto-raised, an alley was the place where you stored your garbage cans and other unsightly things and once in a while a city truck came by, emptied the cans and left those scattered around randomly. But this alley was a quiet private work of art in itself. It was beautiful, and I sat overlooking it all day as I drew comic strips and Crispin and his staff started companies. I had solitude when I wanted it and also someone to go out to lunch with.

Most cartoonists cherish their solitude. I do, too, when I need it. I've spent much of my almost thirty-year career in that solitude. But there is another opportunity when you have people around you, and that is to hone your listening skills. I want to hear what's emotionally meaningful to people. Over time, I've become better at listening to people, which has improved my writing and my strip and my motivational talks to thousands of young people.

After a few years, Crispin and Nora moved out of the cul-de-sac and into a larger house, and Crispin also moved his office to a much larger space. I have nothing to do with his business dealings, but I came along with the other furniture. I had my little private cubicle, a window with nice view, a copier, and a printer. What else does a cartoonist need?

Life Lesson: Appreciate and respect yourself. You are more than a selfie.

We live in a social-media-crazed world, where millions of selfies are on constant display, and vanity and narcissism are celebrated instead of frowned upon. Humility seems all but lost, and the selfie is the antithesis of the humble, complicated, well-meaning, flawed, magnificent reality of you.

Your collage represents the lush complexity of being you. Each day, shortly after waking up, remember that today is another opportunity for you to add something brilliant to your collage, and to your life story.

When you look at your life in the collage you created, you see that you have altered the course of history just by being born. Your birth had an impact on the world. Your existence has an impact upon all of us, even if you have only directly influenced a small number of people.

I MEET MY FATHER, AND ALSO LEARN THE HOLLYWOOD GAME

DRAWING LESSON:
Draw opposites together.

WHAT YOU WILL NEED:
- Flair pen
- Pad of tracing paper

THE LESSON

Opposite personalities being forced to share a small space is the basis of everything from television shows like *The Odd Couple* and *All in the Family* to comics like *Beetle Bailey*, *Calvin and Hobbes*, and even the twins in *JumpStart*.

Opposites are used so often to tell a story because of the conflict that exists between characters who have "nothing in common." The punch lines lie in revealing just how much the apparent "odd" pairing has in common, after all. This same fundamental is behind my creation of Joe and his cop partner, Crunchy.

If Archie and "Meathead" (in *All in the Family*) were both liberals voting for the same politician, the humor would have been harder to come by. If Calvin and Hobbes were both self-centered and non-reflective, there would be nowhere for that comic strip to go.

Think of two extremely different personalities. I recommend using actual people or pets that you know.

Now imagine a situation in which they are forced to spend time together. It can be a job situation or between roommates or some sort of other weird circumstance. Think "stranded on a desert island."

Who are your characters? Animals who think? Are they humans? Aliens or robots? Think outside the box. Come up with some truly original characters. They can be almost anything as long as the average person can relate to them.

Before drawing your characters, practice making geometric shapes. Use your tracing paper so you can shift the layers of ovals over the drawings of squares. Something happens when peering through overlapping layers of shapes as you move the tracing paper sheets around on top of one another. Characters almost begin to draw themselves.

Once you find overlapping shapes that you feel best define the look of your characters, then work on their facial structures and expressions. It's incredible how much emotion you can extract from a simple line for a mouth and two dots for eyes.

Using your tracing paper, work on the structure of the hands, the feet, the posture of each one of your characters. This is a long process. Cartooning is not a shortcut through the world of art. But it is always fun!

Use your tracing paper to make final versions of your characters from the front, back, and profile.

It should be obvious, just by looking at your characters that they are, in fact, opposites for one another. At a glance, Felix Unger looks like a neat-freak, and Oscar Madison appears to be a slob. Remember, that's the underlying tension in *The Odd Couple*.

Finally, name your characters. You now have the basis of a comic strip, book, television show, or anything else in which opposites can entertain.

MY LIFE: WILLIAM ARMSTRONG DABBLES IN FATHERHOOD. I DABBLE IN ACTING.

Thanksgiving 2010 was a special holiday. My relatives back in Philadelphia had rented out the Girl Scouts lodge in Roxborough, a neighborhood in Northwest Philadelphia. Crystal and I flew out from California. The lodge was in a beautiful setting, surrounded by trees and just across the road from a big golf course.

A surprise guest was there, too. A man I'd seen before but never spoken to. William Armstrong had abandoned his family about the time I was born, and I'd seen him only occasionally as a child. He had been ignoring me for forty-eight years by now, and I could return the favor.

But Crystal, in her special way of relating and helping others relate, told me to go talk to him. I walked outside to where William was smoking a cigarette. He was apparently in a mood for unburdening himself.

"I've been meaning to talk to you," he said. "I'm your father. I know I've never acted like your father. I've never checked on you." He pulled out a wad of money from his pocket, crumpled up hundred-dollar bills. He continued, "I don't want anything from you. I've got my own money. I can understand why you hate me so much."

"I don't hate you," I said. "I don't even know you."

"Call me Dad. I want to start acting like your dad."

"I'm forty-eight. You were never around, never my dad when I needed a dad. I'll call you my father."

My parents' wedding in 1951. This is my only photo of them together.

William wanted to do "fatherly" things with me and asked me how to do that. I suggested we go to a basketball game together. He bought some tickets but then canceled the day of the game, saying he had something else to do that day. I used his tickets to take my son to the game. Think about the irony of that. He had made—after forty-eight years—an effort to become the "dad" I had never had, only to give up immediately and revert to his old self. I suppose all this was hard for him, and perhaps he deserves some small credit for trying, however feebly. We spoke a few times by telephone, stilted father-son conversations. He was living in Florida and, by 2012, was very sick and being taken care of by my sister Judi. He died that year, and Judi buried him.

So I had a father for two years. Sort of. Can't say he had much influence on my life other than as an example not to follow when it came to child-rearing.

Meanwhile, back in Los Angeles, I was trying to jump-start some action on *JumpStart*. It was a good time for it, as it happened. In 2011 United Feature Syndicate turned over syndication management of its comic strips to a company called Universal Uclick, which was a part of Andrews McMeel Universal. Universal Uclick already had *Doonesbury*, *Ziggy*, *Cathy* and many other strips in its inventory, but now it had hundreds more, including my *JumpStart*. Soon after, I got a call from Bridget McMeel.

Inking over my roughs onto tracing paper, a three-hour process. This is what I was working on when Bridget McMeel called.

Bridget McMeel.

Bridget was a partner in Andrews McMeel (the titular McMeel being her father) and also ran Amuse, a subsidiary that bills itself as "Extending the presence of Our Creators into the Television and Film Industries." And Bridget had great ideas for *JumpStart*.

Bridget has an effervescent personality. Her sparkling eyes and upbeat personality perfectly bridge the gap between comic strips and electronic entertainment. She's one of the most positive people I have ever met. Hollywood is familiar territory to Bridget, and our first order of business was to secure an agent at one of the big talent agencies.

By this time, I was already eager to get the ball rolling in Hollywood. In fact, before I had even moved to LA, I had tried to get some television shows or movies on the air.

For example, in 2008, my friend, stand-up comedian and actor Tommy Davidson, had invited me and my wife to join him in Hawaii. He called it a wedding gift (since Crystal and I had been married the year before).

Tommy had rented a collection of bungalows on Oahu, a truly beautiful setting, and he introduced me to some locals, a mother and two daughters, friends of his. Tommy suggested that we do a television show about those girls. That night I wrote up a concept about a family who moved from Queens, New York, to Hawaii and called it *Aloha Queens*. At breakfast the next morning I pitched that to Tommy, and he said, "You totally did it."

So far as I was concerned, my work was over. I was wrong. Tommy and I tried and tried to figure out how to make *Aloha Queens* happen. It never did.

Next, and shortly after I moved to LA, I met Bruce Economou through an associate of Tommy Davidson, and we hit it off. Bruce was a tall, good-looking guy with sandy hair and very personable. He moved with precision and had a methodical approach to things. Bruce was an actor before becoming a manager. (It seemed to me that half the people I met in Los Angeles were actors—I even became one, briefly.) Bruce liked me and saw the potential in turning *JumpStart* into a movie or television show. But I needed someone to manage my career and help me navigate the West Coast.

Bruce arranged for me to meet with Matt Alvarez, a young Hollywood producer and executive who had been largely responsible for Ice Cube's stardom. Matt could make things happen, and I was excited to be given the opportunity to pitch him.

Just weeks earlier, my speaking engagement manager had booked me to appear at The Buckley School, a prestigious private school in Sherman Oaks, where many celebrities send their kids. I managed to speak to the entire school in one day, middle school and also the older kids. The little kids, especially, were just giddy over my talk. Afterward, a woman walked up to me and said, "I'm a parent but also a manager for celebrities. Do you have representation?" She was Wendi Niad, and I sort of fumbled around for a moment, taken aback.

"Yes," I said. "Bruce Economou. Why?"

"Well, you have real presence, real confidence up there. I've never seen any-one hold the attention of a bunch of little kids in kindergarten, and also their parents and teachers. We should get together for talks."

We did. Right then. Over coffee, Wendi told me her vision of a *JumpStart* tele-vision show, movie, and a book collection. Listening to Wendi talk of her vision for my career was refreshing and exciting. For once, I wasn't the one trying to convince someone else of my ambitious hopes and dreams. Wendi was telling me all the same stuff I wanted to be telling other people. I said, "I guess I'll hire you."

So I had to release Bruce. Bruce was a nice guy and a great manager with lot of successful clients. But he wasn't a good fit for me. I met with him and gave him the bad news. He took it oddly, I thought.

"Doing this in person shows integrity," Bruce said. "That's important in any-thing you do." Bruce said I was special because of that. It didn't seem that special to me. If there's one easy lesson from this, it's to handle your difficult business face-to-face.

Wendi and I met Matt Alvarez at his CubeVision office in West Hollywood. Ice Cube was in another room, but I could hear his distinctive voice booming from down the hallway. I loved feeling like this was the big time. My transition from cartoonist to executive producer seemed imminent. Matt said they were working on selling another show, *Are We There Yet?*, and that, once that deal was complete, he would be able to focus on *JumpStart*.

Wendi Niad.

Wendi was aggressive. When Matt Alvarez said he had put *JumpStart* in line behind *Are We There Yet?*, Wendi wasn't happy. Wendi told me that she knew of some people who wanted to jump on this. Jump on *JumpStart*, I guess. She set up some meetings. Not all worked. She arranged meetings with Martin Lawrence's company, Runtel-dat, and with Jamie Foxx's company, FoxxKing. Marcus King was the pro-ducer/manager who had helped make Jamie Foxx a well-known television star and produced, among other things, the *Jamie Foxx Show*.

Wendi and I met with Darice Rollins at Runteldat in Studio City, across the street from CBS. Darice liked the *JumpStart* property and seemed to hit it off with

Wendi and me. But she later told us that her boss—Martin Lawrence—"wasn't feeling it."

When we went to Jamie Foxx's office, we met Nikita Adams, a stunning Black woman with dreadlocks and a huge smile. She had read the material and seemed raring to go.

Nikita Adams.

Nikita was warm and ebullient, and her interest in *JumpStart* seemed to be immediate. By meeting's end, we had practically signed a contract. She envisioned it all: television show, both animated and live-action movies, even merchandise. It was an extremely successful meeting—or so I thought.

I seemed now to have options: Ice Cube or Jamie Foxx. Wendi asked me who I wanted to work with. She reminded me that only one of these men had an Oscar. I was seriously being asked to make that choice! After long thought, I settled on FoxxKing.

Shortly after meeting Nikita, and midway through our tour of meetings with Hollywood producers, Wendi sent me on my first television audition. I think the theory was for me to learn more about the business, to feel like a "player," and to get some positive reaction, if possible.

Needless to say, I was insecure. I still had not yet come to think of myself as a Hollywood guy, let alone an actor. I remember showing up for my first audition—as some sort of truck driver—wearing what I thought were truck driver clothes and a baseball cap. It was for a new Nickelodeon show called *Supah Ninjas.*

I was all prepped and excited. I had spent two days memorizing my lines, delivering them in front of a mirror. That felt weird and unnatural, so I developed my own backstory for this truck driver. I imagined he was Italian. His truck would have broken down in front of the building where I would audition. He'd walk in dressed like a truck driver, asking to use a phone, and someone would abruptly invite him to read for a part on a kids' television show. Sure. That could happen—it was Hollywood, after all. I guess that was the Robb Armstrong school of acting.

I showed up at the right place at the right time and all prepped. Barbara

Clothier would have been proud; I was on time and dressed to make an impression. The auditions were in a small room, and actors shuffled in and out in almost a steady line. My turn came. I shuffled in wearing my trucker's hat, flannel plaid shirt, jeans, and boots. Two white women were in the room, one who operated a camera pointed at the door and never spoke, the other who sat on a sofa. I stood somewhat uncomfortably in front of the woman on the sofa. She asked me for my headshot. I didn't have a professional head shot. I barely knew what a head shot was. On the way to the audition, I had stopped at a FedEx Office and printed a photo I had on my phone. It was on flimsy paper.

"Nobody is going to say, 'action,'" the woman said. "Give us your name for the slate." I did so. "Now turn profile to both sides." I did that, too. "Now say your lines," she said.

She looked up and said, "Take off the hat."

"It's part of my costume," I said.

"We get it. Take it off."

I did my little speech, only a few words. She said, "Thank you."

And I put my hat back on and shuffled out, a little disappointed. *That's it?* I thought. *So much for my acting career.*

A half hour later, I was driving home and still reciting my lines, trying various versions and feeling like a loser. My cell phone rang. It was Wendi.

"You booked it!" she said.

"Yep," I said. "At least it's over."

"No, no, no," she said. "You *booked* it. You've won your first acting role on television!"

I couldn't believe it. My first audition was also my first booking.

Wow, this acting stuff is so easy, I thought.

In fact, the first three auditions I went to all resulted in small acting gigs. I went to sixteen more auditions and got—nothing.

Wow. This acting stuff is . . . not so easy.

Still, I learned two valuable things: First, I was really jacked up from the first auditions and the acting work. You need something to keep you moving forward, anything you can grab hold of. At that point in my budding Hollywood career, it was a wonderful thing to have happen.

But, second, acting was only a distraction for me. I already had a job, and attending auditions took a lot of my time. I made a decision. I was a comic-strip artist, not an actor. I didn't need to be an actor; I needed to focus on what had brought me there in the first place.

Life Lesson: Don't let bitterness stunt your growth. And don't let pride stop you from asking for help.

It's okay to be angry for a righteous cause, but letting go of it quickly is what allows you to heal. Was I angry at my father for ignoring me until I was in my forties? At some level, probably yes. But by the time he attempted to come back into my life, he was irrelevant to me. At that family outing in Pennsylvania, I came to realize that I didn't hate my father because I didn't know him that well. I had to get over the differences I had with my father. I realized that he was very ill and that we had to quickly find common ground. And, as it happened, his life would be over within two years. I learned that clinging to hostile feelings was a bad idea; it would have been sinful.

And when I came to Los Angeles to seek out fresh ways to get my comic strip before the public, I was not too proud to ask for help from anyone willing to give it. This now comes naturally to me because I've been asking for—and receiving—help all my life. And I try to repay that generosity wherever I can. That's a part of life, a good part. We give. We take. We share. We pass on those gifts. Why wait for Christmas when you can give someone something useful today? And we all have something we can give away. So don't just stand there; do something nice.

Chapter 19

CALIFORNIA KNOWS HOW TO PARTY

DRAWING LESSON:
Learn image processing.

WHAT YOU WILL NEED:

- Computer
- Adobe Photoshop software (or GIMP)

THE LESSON

This is not an art lesson like the previous ones. This is my way of show-ing you how I use modern technology to complete each strip of *Jump-Start*. Photoshop is as valuable as any paintbrush. My comic strip has been created partially in Photoshop since the early '90s. All the clean-up, gray-scales, and coloring is done in this remarkable software program. Even if you don't buy it right away (it is pricey), it's worth going on line to find out more about it.

If you can't afford Photoshop, then try GIMP, a freeware program that contains a tutorial on how to use it. Both programs are available in both PC and Mac versions.

Photoshop is the drawing of the future. The time will come when most of the art we see will have been created digitally. You can do incredibly artistic things with it. It gives users the ability to enhance existing photos, as we all know, but it also permits them to create drawings from scratch.

For *JumpStart*, I do the initial work in old-fashioned pen and ink, but then I scan the drawing into the computer where, using Photoshop, I can change things, enhance some items, darken a line here or lighten a color there. It's quick and makes the final colors more subtle than I could easily achieve with pen and ink. (And, because the Photoshop colors have specific codes, I can specify, say, Joe's skin tone as a code and the syndicate and the newspapers can replicate that perfectly.)

I'm not advocating that we abandon canvas and paint. But many of today's artists—including filmmakers—are using computer-aided drawing, and knowing what the professionals are up to is useful. The more you know how to use the old tools *and* the new, the better artist you can be.

My Life: The Conga Room at LA Live

It was not all work and no play when I moved from Philadelphia to the West Coast. There were lots of parties: Oscar parties, Super Bowl parties, parties celebrating . . . Monday. Some of my new friends had pools and friends who were actors. I met so many actors.

Many people in Los Angeles share similar goals and ambitions. It is unlike any place I have ever lived. In Philadelphia, a person's occupation was never a distracting topic of conversation, but in LA it seemed to dominate every conversation. Often, the climb toward fame or fortune was the entire point of the party itself. So many people I met looked at me as if to examine me. Was I somebody in the business? Was I someone who could help them?

I began to feel like a big shot because I had made a deal with FoxxKing. Sometimes I'd mention it and feel something wash over me. It was the intoxicating feeling of Hollywood success. Or maybe it was the tequila. Suddenly I was raising a glass, toasting my own success with increasing regularity.

One of the perks of being in the FoxxKing family was cutting loose with Jamie Foxx and his business partner Marcus King. They had an arrangement with a nightclub called the Conga Room at LA Live. LA Live is a metropolis of nightlife carved into the epicenter of downtown Los Angeles, sharing a massive plaza with the Staples Center and the Nokia Theater. And every Monday night at the Conga Room belonged to FoxxKing. It was an intimate venue where talent would appear onstage and sing, dance, rap, or do stand-up comedy. Acts didn't seem to be publicized beforehand in any way, which helped the Conga Room maintain its hot-spot vibe. You just never knew who would appear onstage and light the place up. One night, Busta Rhymes jumped up there. Stevie Wonder made a surprise appearance. It was, for some, a chance for a big break. An unknown would get up there and shock everybody. It was a blast!

I had special connections and a front-table seat in a room designed to be standing room only for eighty percent of the audience.

Some of the many party people in LA.

Life was good. But my deal with FoxxKing seemed to be moving too slowly toward television. And, as fun as it was to be around famous people, I had greater aspirations than hanging out at the Conga Room.

Marcus King knew I was getting antsy and kept me interested by inviting me to be a special guest on *The Foxxhole* radio show, or by participating in an occasional reality-show pilot. But I was becoming concerned that Jamie Foxx was rarely in the office when I was there.

Nikita was wonderful to work with, though, and began interviewing writers to run my show. We settled on a showrunner (that's the writer, producer, and organizer for the show) named Kriss Turner, who had a long list of credits including producing episodes of *The First Family* and *Everybody Hates Chris* and writing on *The Bernie Mac Show*, *Living Single* and *The Soul Man*, among much else.

I met Kriss at the FoxxKing office, but she felt uncomfortable writing there. Nikita and I would instead work with Kriss in Kriss's home high in the Hollywood

Kriss Turner.

Hills, right under the famous Hollywood sign. It was almost eerie to see that massive sign so close to her house.

And what a house it was. An ultramodern glass-and-wood-and-steel structure that hung over a cliff with a view of Hollywood, too dramatic for words. Kriss was nonchalant about her house, telling me more than one time that, "We'd better sell this show so I can buy something better."

Kriss was a smart, careful thinker. She would pace the floor, writing on a giant whiteboard in her dining area. I'd sit at her table, drinking black coffee and sketching drawing after drawing of my *JumpStart* characters, describing their traits and idiosyncrasies.

When I got to Teddy and Tommi, I described them as opposites and said it was a shame the show we were developing wouldn't allow live actors to portray them.

Kriss said we could do it. At that time there was a popular series of television commercials for E*Trade that featured a "talking" live-actor baby. She said we could have talking babies, too, using the same voice-dubbing and facial-manipulation effects used for the E*Trade baby. But soon after, Kriss ditched that idea, thinking it would make the show look cheesy or, worse, like a bad imitation of the E*Trade commercial. I suggested we animate the babies and use real actors for the rest of the cast. They did that, after all, in *Who Framed Roger Rabbit*, with Bob Hoskins talking to an empty space in front of him, where eventually an animated, three-foot rabbit would be placed. Kriss shook her head. The show, she said, would then revolve around wild animated babies who disrupt an otherwise perfect family.

In the end, we had our show structure figured out. The twins would be animated, everyone else played by actors. I created artwork to be used in pitching it to FoxxKing. Even though I was already under contract to FoxxKing there are many steps to getting a television show on the air. Pitches are rehearsed with the producing team before being put on before our agents, FoxxKing's production office agents, then studios, then networks.

Our pitch in the offices of FoxxKing was a huge hit. Marcus loved it. Nikita, who had overseen our project, loved what we had come up with. Jamie Foxx was not in the room, but they assured me they'd show it to him.

Nikita arranged for the team to pitch to Jamie's agents at CAA, the Creative Artists Agency, in order to rehearse before pitching to the networks. The CAA pitch did not go well. For one thing, the agents kept asking why Jamie Foxx wasn't there. As for the show, featuring two animated twins and a live-action cast, the CAA agents felt it was too great a departure from *JumpStart* the comic strip. They suggested we go with total animation and pitch it to Nickelodeon immediately.

But my deal with FoxxKing had expired a week earlier. I hadn't renewed it because I felt we were closing in on something big and I wanted to keep open my options. I could always reconnect with FoxxKing if something good developed. I called Nikita to tell her I would not be signing a new deal, at least not yet, with FoxxKing. Nikita said that she understood.

There were no hard feelings between Nikita and me, and I even invited her to my birthday party a short time later. When she arrived, I went out to the gate to let her in. Before we joined the other guests, she told me that I had made a wise decision by not re-upping with FoxxKing.

"You must be blessed by God," she said. "I'm now unemployed. FoxxKing no longer exists."

Not because of me, I learned. A rift had developed between the partners, and Jamie Foxx parted company with Marcus King.

"Jamie is with Rick Yorn now," Nikita said. "You got out just in time."

About a month later Bridget McMeel called. She set me up to meet Alec Botnick, an agent at William Morris Endeavor.

Alec loved the strip, and we hit it off. So, I became a client of William Morris Endeavor, the world's largest talent agency.

Wendi stayed my manager through this whole process, including the push to go toward animation. She's still my manager.

Alec began the process of looking for producers who could take *JumpStart* to television. We met with a half-dozen and eventually signed with Aaron Kaplan of Kapital Entertainment. Aaron is dynamic and extremely self-confident. At the time that we first met, he was on a winning streak, selling pilots that no one else had been able to blast off. In fact, when we met, he said, "If I can't sell it, it can't be sold."

Next, we had to get a showrunner, a head writer. The chances of selling a show to a big network without a known and top-ranked showrunner were slim.

I chose Andrew Orenstein, who had had tremendous success with *Malcolm in the Middle* and *Everybody Hates Chris*.

The process had been slow. Two years had gone by since my first meetings with Bridget. It took Aaron about a year to set up the writing meetings that led to my partnership with Andrew.

This process was akin to pushing an old wooden cart up the side of a pyramid. Years of pushing upward, wearing me out, but also making me stronger, increasing my endurance. For me, meeting Andrew was like arriving at the pinnacle of that pyramid. Everything that happened after that felt fast, like that cart descending down the other side on its own momentum.

My agent scheduled meetings with all the major networks while Andrew and I met in coffee shops and at my kitchen table, honing and practicing the pitch. We rehearsed delivering the pitch. Finally, after a few months, we were ready to sell the concept of *JumpStart* as a television show for a major network.

CBS passed.

ABC passed.

Nickelodeon didn't go well at all. Andrew felt awful and apologized for blowing it. I said not to worry. We still had the Fox network.

Fox felt good, really good. We pitched Fox on a Friday and by the next Friday, I asked Andrew if he had heard anything about the Fox presentation. It was late in the day, and, frankly, I didn't want to go into the weekend not knowing. I was already suffering from insomnia.

Andrew said, "No one calls Fox. Don't worry about it, Robb. It's out of our hands. Enjoy your weekend."

Ha. That was easy for him to say. I went to Target to fill a prescription, and Aaron called my cell phone as I was standing in line.

"Robb, it's Kap," he said. "Now I know why they push these calls to the end of the day."

My heart sank.

"Unfortunately, you're going to be working with Andrew Orenstein a lot longer," Aaron said. "Fox bought the show."

I began screaming in Target.

"Oh, my God!" I said to Aaron. "We sold it!" This was a culmination of years of work, years of hoping.

I called Bridget and screamed, "Did you hear? We sold to Fox!"

I brought home a bottle of champagne, and Crystal and I celebrated. I called Tess, who had news of her own. She had just landed her first "career job" upon graduating from college. Oh, what a night!

But it was not to be. "Yes," in Hollywood, means "maybe." A promise in Hollywood means nothing. You could wallpaper the inside of Grauman's Chinese

Theatre on Hollywood Boulevard with the signed and sealed contracts that were never actually followed up on.

Both the Fox/*JumpStart* and *Aloha Queens* projects died typical Hollywood deaths. *Aloha Queens* is dormant. *JumpStart* is still considered "in development." It may yet have life as a television show.

It's what happens to the majority of projects. Everyone is enthusiastic and all in favor, and then it goes cold on you. The people who were once wildly enthusiastic about your concept get distracted by the next person's concept and get wildly enthusiastic about that until something else comes along for them to be wildly enthusiastic about. Nothing ever really dies, but projects get put aside, to be revived a decade or more later. Or not at all.

But I'm still working, focused upon getting some sort of movie or television show made from *JumpStart*. There's still Hollywood interest in my strip and I'm always excited about the possibilities. In the meantime, I still do a strip a day, Sundays, too, always meeting deadline. My original dream came true, and I am still delivering on that promise I made to myself at age three and to my mother at age eighteen.

Life Lesson: Diversify.

Look for diversity in your life, and don't just surround yourself with people who agree with you in every way. If you happen to be Black, find a church with white people. Or vice versa. Seek out friendships that tap into the value of diversity. Once inside mixed circles, let your friends express their views, no matter how strange these views may sound to your ears.

You cannot grow from relationships that teach you little or challenge you not at all. When someone very different from you is talking, that's a priceless gift from him to you, so listen without interrupting and be interested.

Chapter 20

...reating a film ...you that will two decades.

what's it called?

"Doctor Appleby"

That's the title?

Yes! It's about a baby whose mother named him "Doctor"

as he grows up, she dresses him in scrubs.

DR. ARMSTRONG, PAGING DR. ARMSTRONG

follow you as embrace this persona...

all the way through college and everything!

How dramatic when I become a physician!

How comedic if you end up becoming something else.

DRAWING LESSON:
Paint with the opposite hand.

WHAT YOU WILL NEED:

- Brushes. Various sizes of sabeline (ox hair) or camel hair high-quality brushes
- Several small jars with lids to put paint into. Save on expensive paint
- Beginner's set of water-based acrylic paints
- 20x30-inch (or larger) canvas pre-stretched over a frame

THE LESSON

Everyone is ambidextrous. If we are able to use both our legs with almost equal effectiveness, then why not our hands? The answer is—because we don't practice it. It simply is not essential to be ambidextrous, so we quickly begin to favor one hand for certain tasks, and the other hand for other tasks.

You will now use your "off hand" to create art! But start by putting some paint into the little jars. Prepare the canvas surface with the gesso, as you did in the earlier lesson about painting over an existing work.

The paintbrush will feel extremely awkward in your off hand. Relax. The way you will move the brush will be easy and fun.

Choose one of the colors and paint some circles on your canvas. Fill those in. If you are right-handed, you are accustomed to pulling the brush to make a circle. Creating a circle with your off hand will be easier if you "push" the brush to make circles. Wait for the circles to dry. Fill in any white spaces between the circles with your remaining colors, always allowing the paint to dry.

You may begin to layer another coat of circles, mixing blue and yellow to make green. Create new circles on top of the old, overlapping, offset, as you wish. Fill in spaces with other shapes: rectangles, squares, triangles, for example. Make purple by mixing red and blue.

Notice something? You are now ambidextrous! You have developed agility in a part of your body you almost never put demands upon. This is a good thing to practice.

The canvas you paint will look surprisingly authentic. You are seeing new possibilities as you apply paint to the surface, and doing so without restrictions.

When you are finished, sign your name with your off hand. It will surprise even you how readable your signature is after all of that practice!

You can have your canvas framed at a do-it-yourself frame shop. You may also buy strips of wood at Home Depot and create a crude frame that is deliberately "shabby chic."

The next canvas you paint with your off hand should be something more recognizable, like a bowl of fruit or a simple landscape. Watching the sun set while painting with your off-hand will allow you to "see" in ways your dominant hand would simply never allow.

MY LIFE: SPEAKING OF PUBLIC SPEAKING . . .

There is no special reason why drawing cartoon strips and public speaking should be intertwined. But, in my life, they are. Perhaps I just like to get out of the house or away from the drawing board at my office.

All of my speaking experience culminated in 2012 when Holy Family University in Philadelphia granted me an honorary doctorate in Humane Letters, honoris causa (for honor or merit). I was stunned. It turned out they had been tracking my work as a cartoonist and also my work as a motivational speaker for young people—mostly, I suspect, the latter.

I planned ahead for my big day. Wrote out my speech. Created a special cartoon for that day. (I do the strips about three weeks in advance and specified the one to run on that particular day.) Not only would the strip run that day in more

Holy Family University 55th Commencement, May 19, 2012. I am being honored with a Doctor of Humane Letters, honoris causa.

than four hundred newspapers, but I also sent it to the university so that it could be added to the commencement program.

At the graduation ceremony, I put on my mortarboard cap and—metaphorically—my humble hat, too. They didn't let me have drawing paper as I usually had for my talks, but I fished out a tattered copy of *JumpStart* from that morning's newspaper and waved that and told the audience to look in their programs for the same one.

I started talking, occasionally distracted by that tassel hanging down in front of my eye. I pointed to my wife, the Hurtigs, the Clothiers, my aunt, my cousins, and others in the audience who had come to cheer me on. I thanked all who had helped me through the years, at Shipley, and in so many other ways. I told the audience:

> For you to give me this honor, you are acknowledging their impact on my life. God put my family, all this large family, around me, not just as a buffer against harm, but truly as a cheerleading squad. They helped to motivate me toward what even to them was a very strange dream. My closest friends and family said, "That's crazy. But don't quit. If anyone can do that, you can. Don't quit." My passion was born here in Philadelphia, and through divine intervention, my passion became reality.
>
> I used to think that talking, speaking in public, was all about me. Turned out it was about the audience, about you. I realized then that my

purpose was to continue doing this, to continue telling audiences about my life and my gratitude to others. You cannot spend your professional life only concerned with yourself. and with becoming personally successful, even prosperous.

Prosperity is often mistaken for success. The resemblance is so strong, the two of them are practically twins. But look a little closer. Success is older and wiser. Success has wrinkles around eyes that weep for the struggles of others. Success has a bloodline that runs through the greatest achievements of humankind. Success is a descendant of Abraham Lincoln and Benjamin Franklin. Martin Luther King Jr. and Frederick Douglass, Leonardo da Vinci, and Mother Teresa. Success can easily trace its roots back to Moses and Jesus Christ. Success, as you can see from this celebrated lineage, isn't always rich. Prosperity, on the other hand, is rolling in it. Success wants company. Prosperity is alone in a crowded room.

It is difficult to meet with Success. You have to get past a bodyguard named Abject Failure.

Failure doesn't just stand in your way. He is willing to be your constant companion for weeks, months, or years. His stamina is formidable as he will stay with you unto death, if necessary. Anything to sift out the dishonest, dispassionate, and weak of character. Failure feasts on quitters. Failure has no remorse, and is not sorry if you never meet with success. Failure knows only one true thing: Success is a far greater burden to bear than Failure. When you are a failure, nobody is counting on you. When you are a success, the whole world is counting on you. Everyone can understand a person who fails. One who succeeds, however, is always misunderstood. Sometimes even assassinated or crucified.

Success is not the story I tell about myself. It is the report given about me by my loved ones.

What will be the report given about you?

It was a heady experience. Some people will say that an honorary doctorate is not a "real" degree. To that I would say that the process leading up to my getting that doctorate was heart wrenching, excruciating, long, and tedious. And it took decades.

Still, I am humbled by it. It's incredible to me. When Holy Family University so honored me, it was a way of saying to me, "Take a break. Stop for a second. Dress up and show up, and let us honor your life work." And so I did. On time, too, since Barbara Clothier was to be there.

My wife, Crystal, teases me when I call to make a dinner reservation at some restaurant. "Tell them you're Doctor Armstrong," she says. I've tried that. It turns out I get the same table either way.

Life Lesson: Be fearless!

Overcoming fear requires action. We often don't experience the fulfillment of life simply because we put limits on what we are willing to try.

But, in my case at least recognizing that God is more powerful than I am not only helped me feel more courageous, but it also gave me the humility I needed to be a useful person in this world.

This book is called *Fearless* not because of my own mind-set but because that is what my mother was. She stood up for her sons. She took on Philadelphia. Did she win? I say yes; she made quite an impression on her youngest child.

I also think back to my brother Billy, his life forever frozen at a young age. He was wild, reckless, and fearless, too. A portion of him lives on in me, his younger brother who often feels that he is soaring off a launching ramp—and with no landing ramp!

EPILOGUE: LIFE GOES ON

Fearlessness is the attribute you will need to unlock the creative potential inside your own mind. I learned to be fearless at the knee of my mother, Dot Armstrong, a woman who bore five children in poverty and went on from working as a seamstress to having a master's degree. There were times I chose courage, other times it was forced upon me, but I always managed to rise to the challenge through the example Dot set and, later, through my faith in God.

I want to add, though, that perseverance is your second most valuable trait. If my life is any example, it's because, despite all odds, I'm still here. I pushed and pushed and pushed until I realized my lifelong dream.

Your dream is different. Your life is different. You have faced and will face entirely different challenges and fears. But be of good cheer; stick-to-itiveness and courage will eventually win the day for you, too.

Now—and this is the last lesson in the book—I want you to ask yourself, as I asked the audience at Holy Family University: When you get to Heaven, what will be the report given about you?

* * *

And thank you, God, for making this kid from West Philadelphia fearless!

ART SUPPLIES

You can buy may of these items in local stores and I like to shop at those cheap Family Dollar–type places. If you can find it there, why pay more? For specialty things I like Michaels, a nationwide chain of art supply stores. Google them for a store near you.

Specialty art supplies aren't cheap but buy quality. If you're just starting out in drawing, hampering yourself with poor brushes or bad paints is just going to discourage you.

Now for a short list of items you need for this book's art lessons. This is the entire list so that you can take it with you to the store but, within each chapter, I'll also list those specific items needed.

- **Flair pen.** Black. Ball-point pens are no good. Flair is a brush-type that goes on wet and dries almost instantly.

- **Sharpie pen,** black at least but if you see a set of colors, get that too. Like Flairs, this is a quick-drying brush-type but quite large.

- **Charcoal pencils.** Black at least but go ahead and buy a color set. Despite the "charcoal" name they now come in various colors.

- **Pastel crayons or Conté crayons.** Set of colors.

- **Beginner's set of water-based acrylic paints.** To start, just buy one basic color (not neon) "paint pot" set.

- **Brushes.** Various sizes of sabeline (ox hair) or camel hair high-quality brushes. You want small, medium, large tip. This is one place to not go cheap as cheap brushes tend to lose hairs that end up stuck to your painting.

- **Gesso** ("jesso"). Thin white paste you spread on surfaces to cover up what's beneath or just to prepare a canvas for paint. It fills in the pores of the canvas and makes colors painted on top brighter. Apply in thin layers and let dry between. Use just enough to get the job done. You want some that works with acrylics. You can buy it by the gallon but an 8-ounce jar should do for starters.

- **Spray fixative,** matte, not gloss. Small spray can of this will protect your charcoal and other artwork.

- **Pad of tracing paper,** 11x14-inch or larger and larger is better. I use 14x17 sheets. Comes in pads or boxes of loose sheets from 50 to 500. One brand comes in a roll, like paper towels. Buy a small quantity (50 or so) to start.

- **Pad of drawing paper.** Suitable for charcoal and pen-and-ink. Comes in pads, often spiral-bound so you keep all your drawings together. I use a 24x36-inch pad but just get the largest size you can find in the art supply store. Strathmore paper is very good.

- **Pad of lined paper.** Sold in stores everywhere.

- **20x30-inch** (or larger) canvas pre-stretched over a frame. Ask for this at the art supply store.

- **Modeling clay.** Buy a few pounds. You can also buy a clay-sculpting set but for our lessons you can get by with kitchen items. You'll also want some resealable plastic bags to keep clay in so it doesn't dry out.

- **Foam board.** Buy several in 24x36-inch size or larger. Color doesn't matter. Don't buy the cork version, it's more fragile and it generates tiny cork dust.

- **A shadow box** without glass large enough for one of your foam boards.

- **Small jars** with lids to put paint into. Save on expensive paint.

JUMPSTART GALLERY

This book was never meant to be a simple collection of _JumpStart_ comic strips, but I know my readers. They want a collection of comic strips. So here are some of my favorite installments of _JumpStart_, in somewhat chronological order. You will quickly notice that not many of my favorites include work from the early years of the strip, which was launched in 1989. I feel that it took some time to find my groove and establish a large cast of diverse, believable characters. There will likely be glaring omissions . . . storylines and individual strips that may have touched you in some way or made it to your fridge (the highest honor there is, for a cartoonist). Send them to me at robb@robbarmstrong.com, and I will include them in my next book.

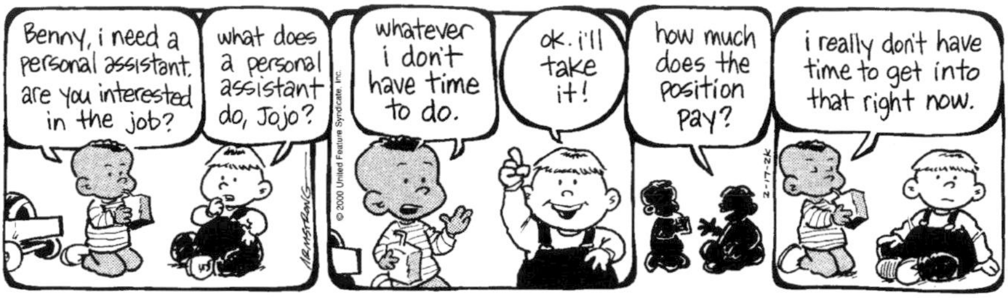
Benny, i need a personal assistant. are you interested in the job?
what does a personal assistant do, Jojo?
whatever i don't have time to do.
ok. i'll take it!
how much does the position pay?
i really don't have time to get into that right now.
© 2000 United Feature Syndicate, Inc.

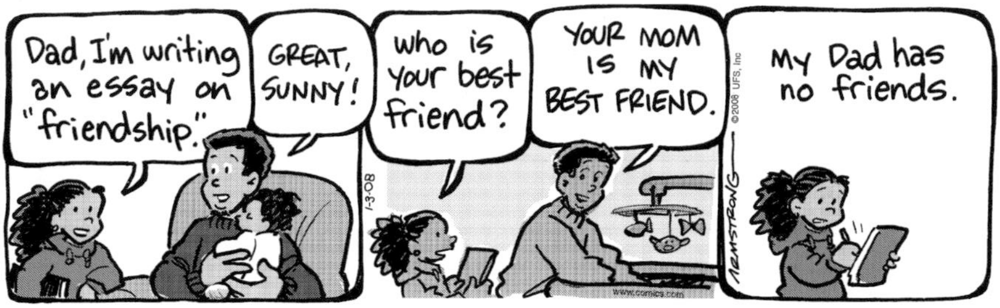
Dad, I'm writing an essay on "friendship."
GREAT, SUNNY!
who is your best friend?
YOUR MOM IS MY BEST FRIEND.
My Dad has no friends.
©2008 UFS, Inc.

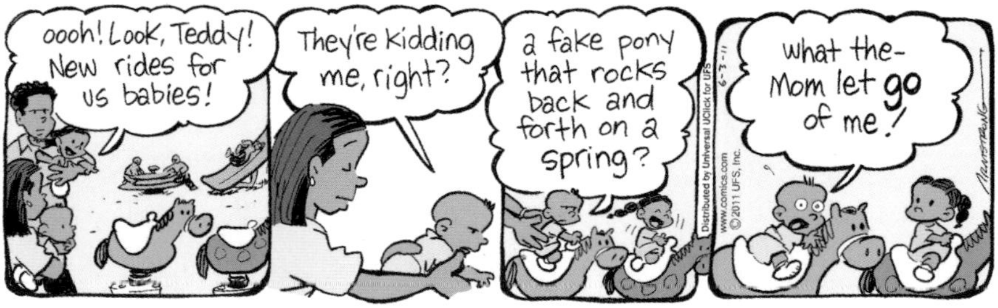
oooh! Look, Teddy! New rides for us babies!
They're kidding me, right?
a fake pony that rocks back and forth on a spring?
what the- Mom let go of me!
Distributed by Universal UClick for UFS
www.comics.com
© 2011 UFS, Inc.

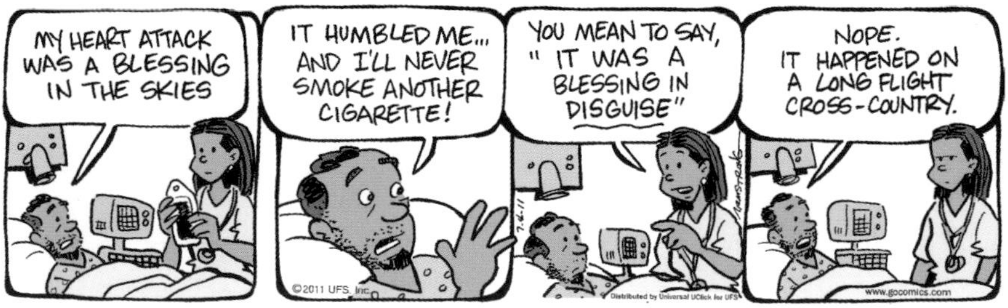
MY HEART ATTACK WAS A BLESSING IN THE SKIES
IT HUMBLED ME... AND I'LL NEVER SMOKE ANOTHER CIGARETTE!
YOU MEAN TO SAY, "IT WAS A BLESSING IN DISGUISE"
NOPE. IT HAPPENED ON A LONG FLIGHT CROSS-COUNTRY.
©2011 UFS, Inc.
www.gocomics.com

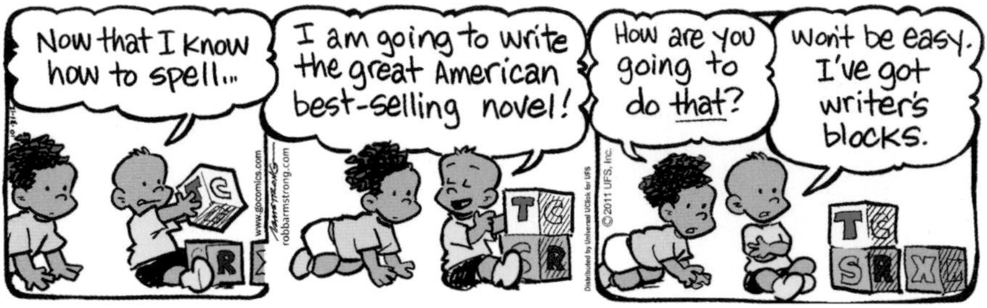
Now that I know how to spell...
I am going to write the great American best-selling novel!
How are you going to do that?
Won't be easy. I've got writer's blocks.

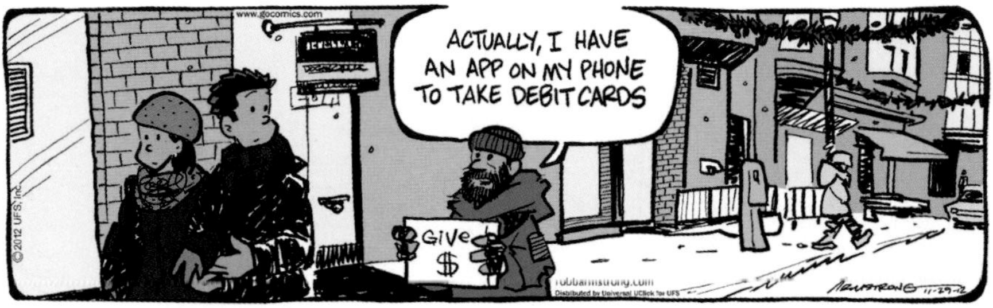
ACTUALLY, I HAVE AN APP ON MY PHONE TO TAKE DEBIT CARDS
GIVE $

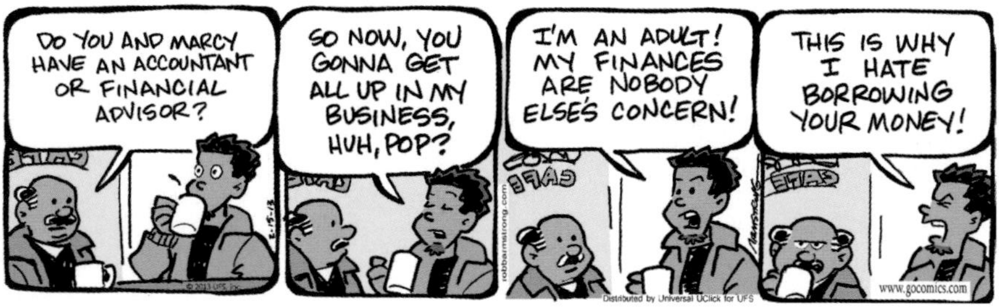
DO YOU AND MARCY HAVE AN ACCOUNTANT OR FINANCIAL ADVISOR?
SO NOW, YOU GONNA GET ALL UP IN MY BUSINESS, HUH, POP?
I'M AN ADULT! MY FINANCES ARE NOBODY ELSE'S CONCERN!
THIS IS WHY I HATE BORROWING YOUR MONEY!

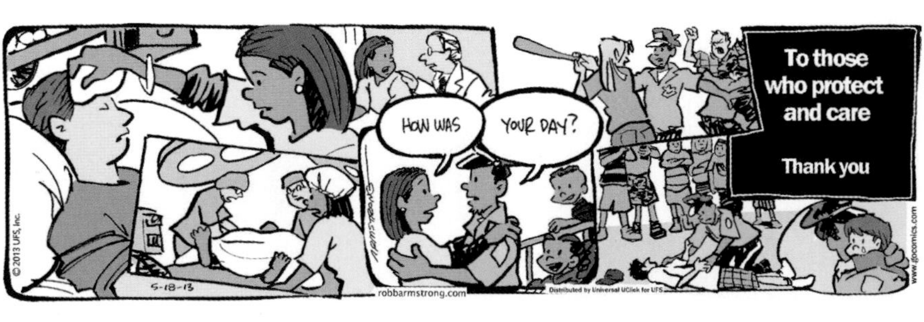
HOW WAS
YOUR DAY?
To those who protect and care
Thank you

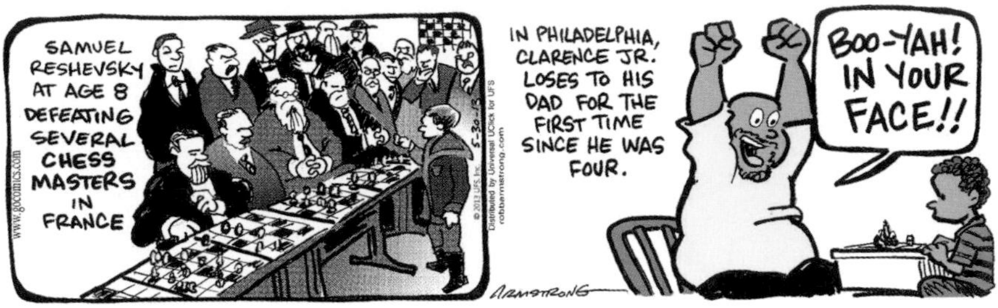
SAMUEL RESHEVSKY AT AGE 8 DEFEATING SEVERAL CHESS MASTERS IN FRANCE
IN PHILADELPHIA, CLARENCE JR. LOSES TO HIS DAD FOR THE FIRST TIME SINCE HE WAS FOUR.
BOO-YAH! IN YOUR FACE!!
www.gocomics.com
Distributed by Universal UClick for UFS
robbarmstrong.com
ARMSTRONG

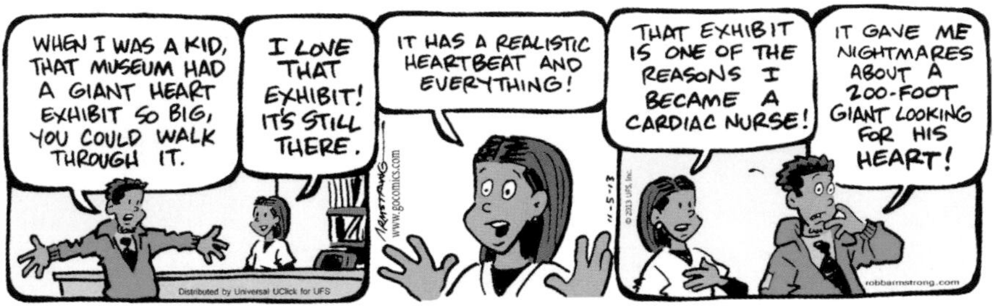
WHEN I WAS A KID, THAT MUSEUM HAD A GIANT HEART EXHIBIT SO BIG, YOU COULD WALK THROUGH IT.
I LOVE THAT EXHIBIT! IT'S STILL THERE.
IT HAS A REALISTIC HEARTBEAT AND EVERYTHING!
THAT EXHIBIT IS ONE OF THE REASONS I BECAME A CARDIAC NURSE!
IT GAVE ME NIGHTMARES ABOUT A 200-FOOT GIANT LOOKING FOR HIS HEART!
Distributed by Universal UClick for UFS
www.gocomics.com
robbarmstrong.com

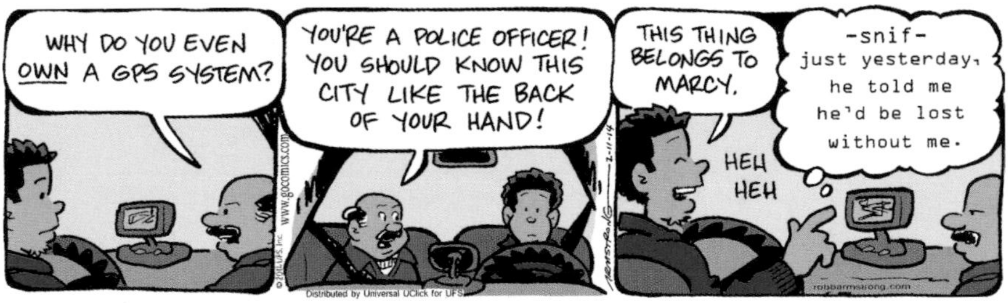
WHY DO YOU EVEN OWN A GPS SYSTEM?
YOU'RE A POLICE OFFICER! YOU SHOULD KNOW THIS CITY LIKE THE BACK OF YOUR HAND!
THIS THING BELONGS TO MARCY.
HEH HEH
-snif- just yesterday, he told me he'd be lost without me.
www.gocomics.com
Distributed by Universal UClick for UFS
robbarmstrong.com

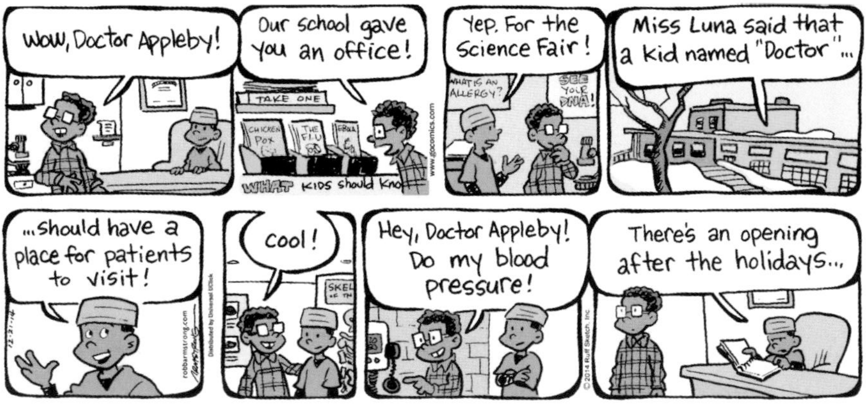
Wow, Doctor Appleby!
Our school gave you an office!
TAKE ONE
WHAT KIDS should Know
Yep. For the Science Fair!
WHAT IS AN ALLERGY?
SEE YOUR DNA!
Miss Luna said that a kid named "Doctor"...
...should have a place for patients to visit!
Cool!
Hey, Doctor Appleby! Do my blood pressure!
There's an opening after the holidays...
www.gocomics.com
robbarmstrong.com

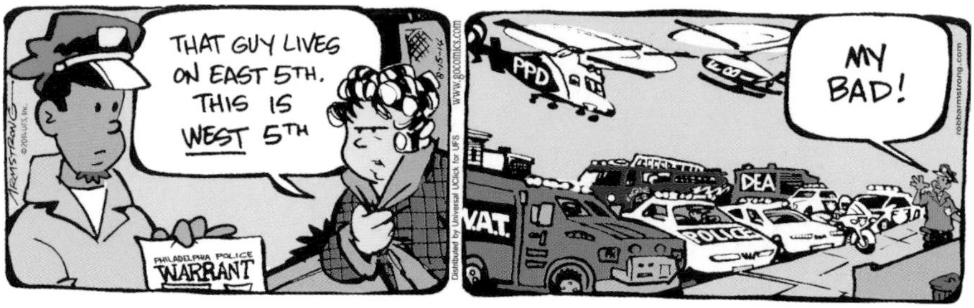
THAT GUY LIVES ON EAST 5TH. THIS IS WEST 5TH
PHILADELPHIA POLICE WARRANT
MY BAD!
PPD
DEA
POLICE
www.gocomics.com
Distributed by Universal UClick for UFS
robbarmstrong.com

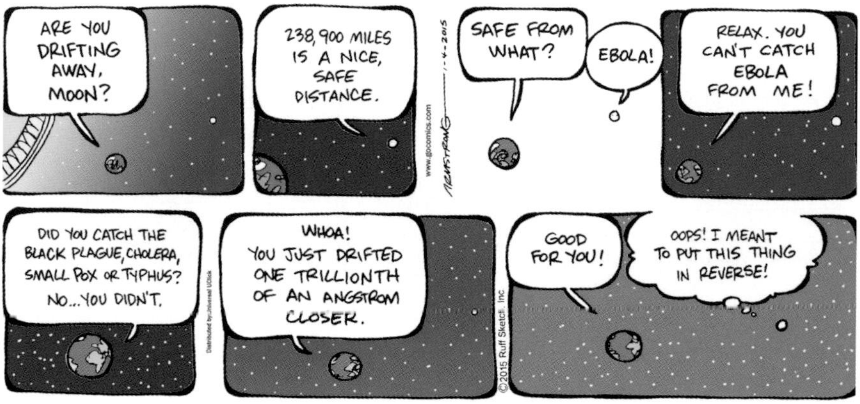
ARE YOU DRIFTING AWAY, MOON?
238,900 MILES IS A NICE, SAFE DISTANCE.
SAFE FROM WHAT?
EBOLA!
RELAX. YOU CAN'T CATCH EBOLA FROM ME!
DID YOU CATCH THE BLACK PLAGUE, CHOLERA, SMALL POX OR TYPHUS? NO... YOU DIDN'T.
WHOA! YOU JUST DRIFTED ONE TRILLIONTH OF AN ANGSTROM CLOSER.
GOOD FOR YOU!
OOPS! I MEANT TO PUT THIS THING IN REVERSE!
www.gocomics.com
©2015 Ruff Sketch, Inc.

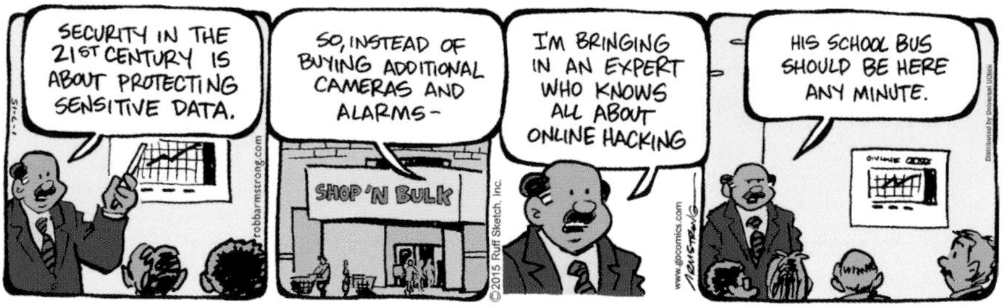
SECURITY IN THE 21ST CENTURY IS ABOUT PROTECTING SENSITIVE DATA.
SO, INSTEAD OF BUYING ADDITIONAL CAMERAS AND ALARMS-
SHOP 'N BULK
I'M BRINGING IN AN EXPERT WHO KNOWS ALL ABOUT ONLINE HACKING
HIS SCHOOL BUS SHOULD BE HERE ANY MINUTE.
robbarmstrong.com
©2015 Ruff Sketch, Inc.
www.gocomics.com

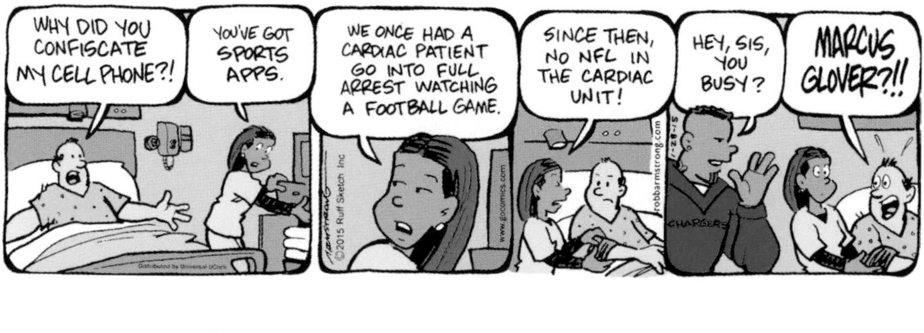
WHY DID YOU CONFISCATE MY CELL PHONE?!
YOU'VE GOT SPORTS APPS.
WE ONCE HAD A CARDIAC PATIENT GO INTO FULL ARREST WATCHING A FOOTBALL GAME.
SINCE THEN, NO NFL IN THE CARDIAC UNIT!
HEY, SIS, YOU BUSY?
MARCUS GLOVER?!!
CHARGERS
©2015 Ruff Sketch Inc
www.gocomics.com
robbarmstrong.com

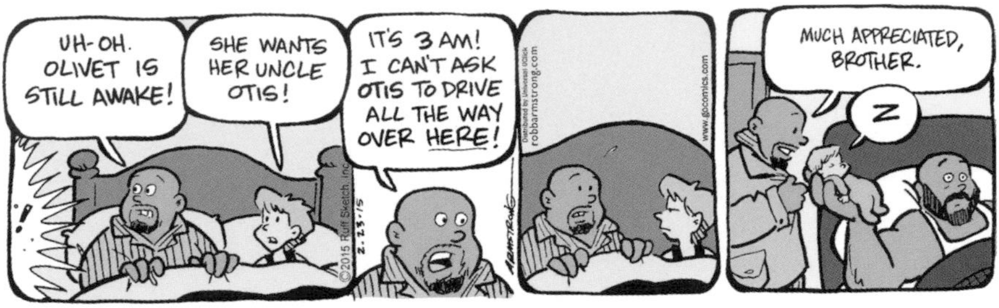
UH-OH. OLIVET IS STILL AWAKE!
SHE WANTS HER UNCLE OTIS!
IT'S 3 AM! I CAN'T ASK OTIS TO DRIVE ALL THE WAY OVER HERE!
MUCH APPRECIATED, BROTHER.
Z

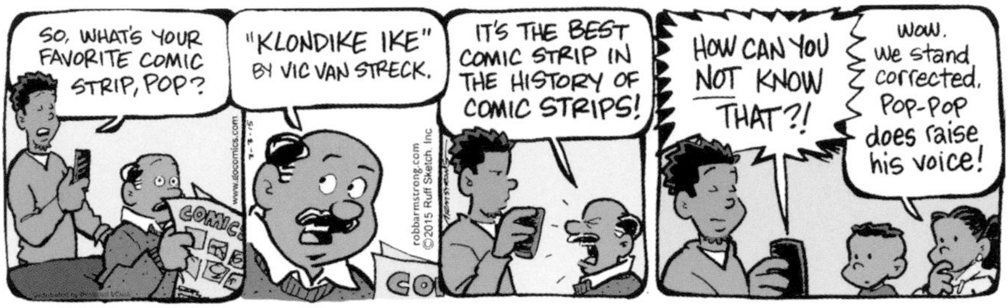
SO, WHAT'S YOUR FAVORITE COMIC STRIP, POP?
COMICS
"KLONDIKE IKE" BY VIC VAN STRECK.
IT'S THE BEST COMIC STRIP IN THE HISTORY OF COMIC STRIPS!
HOW CAN YOU NOT KNOW THAT?!
WOW. We stand corrected. Pop-Pop does raise his voice!

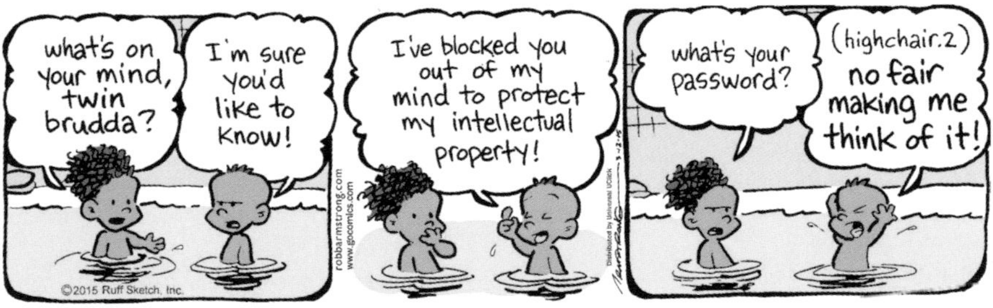
what's on your mind, twin brudda?
I'm sure you'd like to know!
I've blocked you out of my mind to protect my intellectual property!
what's your password?
(highchair.2) no fair making me think of it!

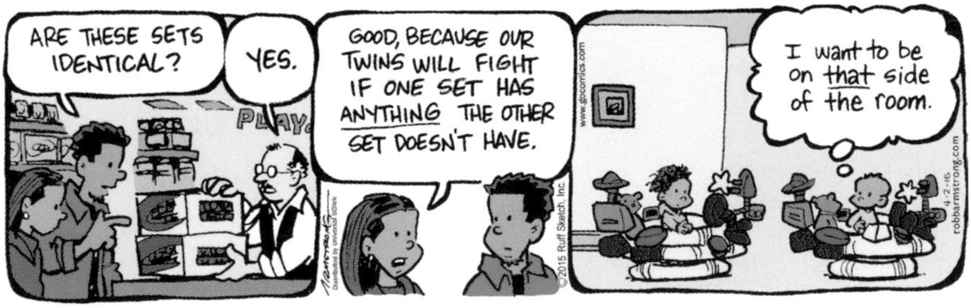
ARE THESE SETS IDENTICAL?
YES.
PLAY
GOOD, BECAUSE OUR TWINS WILL FIGHT IF ONE SET HAS ANYTHING THE OTHER SET DOESN'T HAVE.
I want to be on that side of the room.

INDEX

B

C

D

E

F

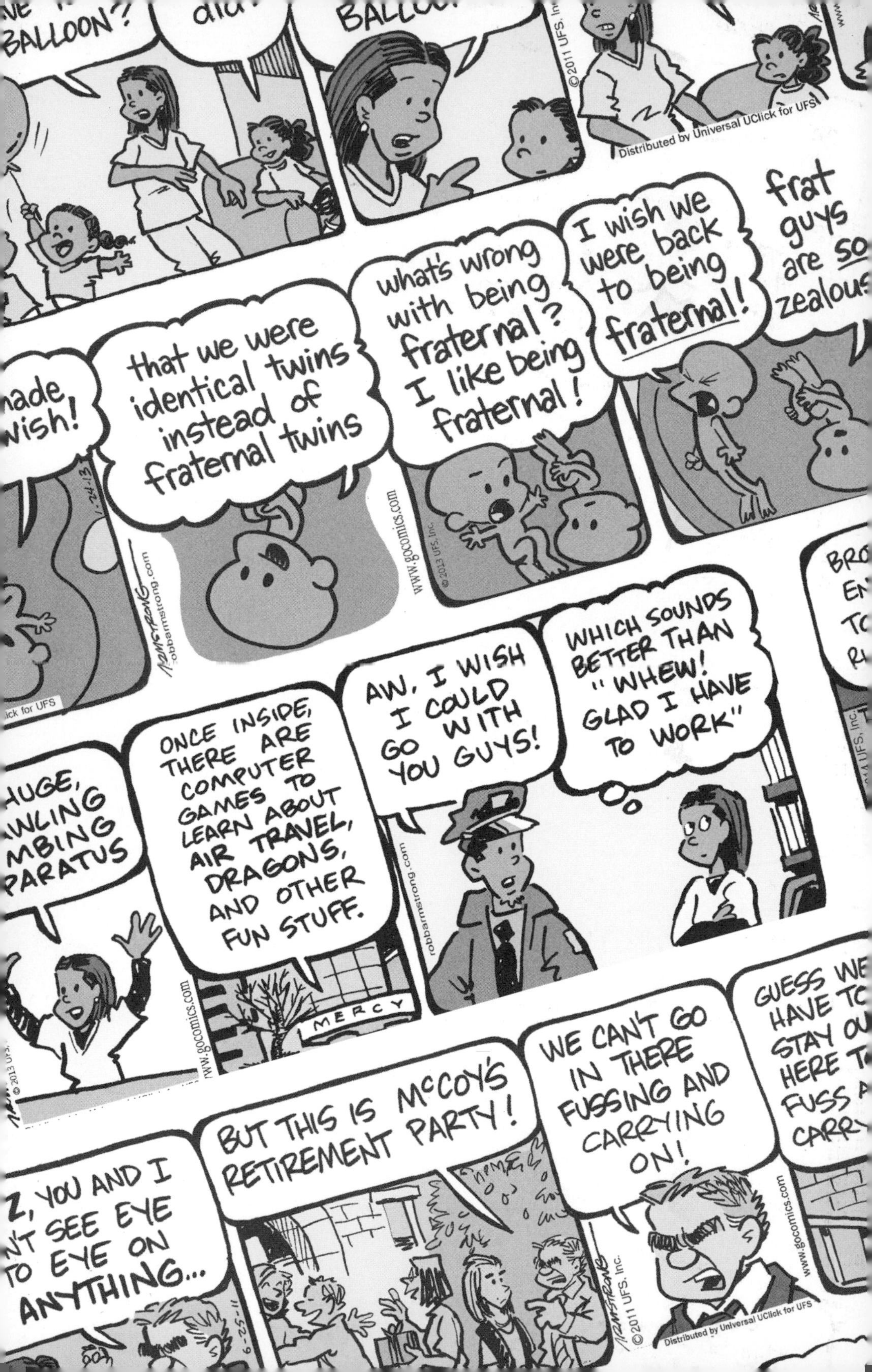

BALLOON?
©2011 UFS, Inc.
Distributed by Universal UClick for UFS
made wish!
that we were identical twins instead of fraternal twins
1-24-13
robbarmstrong.com
what's wrong with being fraternal? I like being fraternal!
© 2013 UFS, Inc.
www.gocomics.com
I wish we were back to being fraternal!
frat guys are so zealous
HUGE,
MBING
PARATUS
ONCE INSIDE, THERE ARE COMPUTER GAMES TO LEARN ABOUT AIR TRAVEL, DRAGONS, AND OTHER FUN STUFF.
© 2013 UFS
www.gocomics.com
MERCY
AW, I WISH I COULD GO WITH YOU GUYS!
robbarmstrong.com
WHICH SOUNDS BETTER THAN "WHEW! GLAD I HAVE TO WORK"
YOU AND I
SEE EYE TO EYE ON ANYTHING...
BUT THIS IS McCOY'S RETIREMENT PARTY!
6-25-11
© 2011 UFS, Inc.
WE CAN'T GO IN THERE FUSSING AND CARRYING ON!
www.gocomics.com
Distributed by Universal UClick for UFS
GUESS WE HAVE TO STAY OU HERE TO FUSS A CARRY